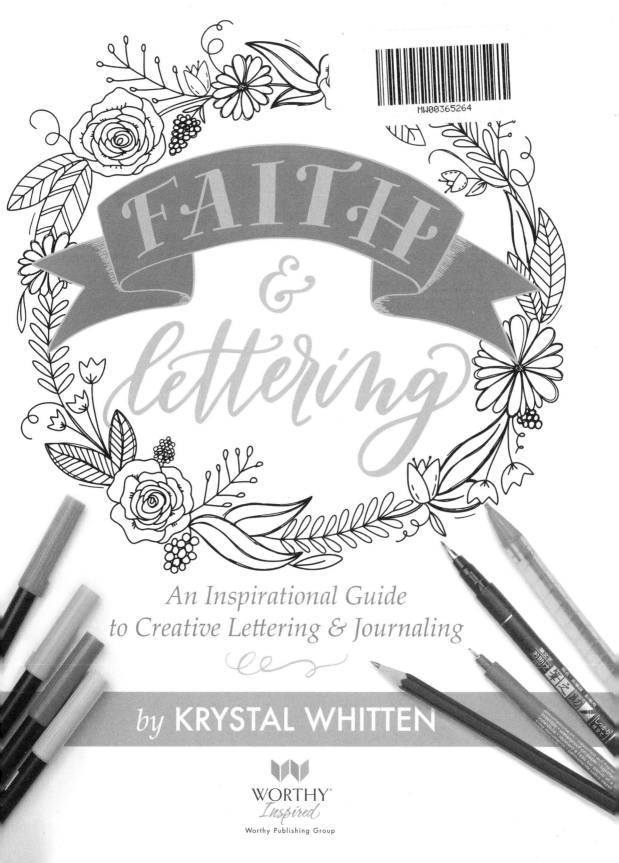

FAITH & lettering

An Inspirational Guide
to Creative Lettering & Journaling

by KRYSTAL WHITTEN

WORTHY®
Inspired
Worthy Publishing Group

Faith and Lettering : An Inspirational Guide to Creative Lettering and Journaling

Copyright © 2018 by Krystal Whitten
Published by Worthy Inspired, an imprint of Worthy Publishing Group, a division of
Worthy Media, Inc., One Franklin Park, 6100 Tower Circle, Suite 210, Franklin, TN 37067.

WORTHY is a registered trademark of Worthy Media, Inc.
Helping people experience the heart of God

Library of Congress Control Number: 2017960788

Published in association with the literary agency of Legacy, LLC, 501 N. Orlando Avenue, Suite
#313-348, Winter Park, FL 32789.

For foreign and subsidiary rights, contact rights@worthypublishing.com

ISBN: 978-1-68397-243-3

Photos: Krystal Whitten, Laura Foote, Ben Griffin
Cover Design: Krystal Whitten
Interior Design and Typesetting: Jeff Jansen | Aesthetic Soup

Printed in the United States of America

18 19 20 21 22 — 10 9 8 7 6 5 4 3 2

Contents

Dedication 1

Introduction to Faith and Lettering 2

Section 1 – Lettering Basics 9

    Chapter 1: Terms and Tools 11

    Chapter 2: Let's Start Lettering 21

    Chapter 3: Modern Calligraphy 43

Section 2 – Creative Elements 63

    Chapter 4: Ribbon Banners 65

    Chapter 5: Flowers 73

    Chapter 6: Wreaths 81

    Chapter 7: Flourishes and Frames 89

Section 3 – Layout and Technique 103

    Chapter 8: Putting It All Together 105

    Chapter 9: Just Start 117

Section 4 – Faith Journaling 127

    Chapter 10: Creative Sermon Notes 129

    Chapter 11: Bible Journaling 143

Section 5 – Lettering with a Purpose 153

    Chapter 12: Lifestyle Lettering 155

    Chapter 13: Lettering for the Lord 165

About the Author/Where to Follow 171

dedicated to

MY HUSBAND ANDY -
Without your encouragement and support,
this book would never have come to be.

MY LORD JESUS CHRIST -
May You be glorified in everything I do.

Introduction

What Is Faith and Lettering?

Where It All Began

I was twelve years old, sitting on my hot-pink bedspread, surrounded by notebook paper, and chewing the cap of a Magic Marker. I loved handwriting, but I didn't like *my* handwriting. I was intent on changing the way I wrote. As I looked at a penmanship book for reference, I carefully copied the letters over and over. I practiced by writing the lyrics to my favorite song and, pleased with the results, I taped my work to a wall in my bedroom. My walls became papered with Scriptures, poems, and more lyrics. I exchanged elaborately styled notes with friends and decorated their names with curlicues and dots. I loved lettering before I knew it was a real thing.

But I left behind my "childish" drawing when I got to college. I traded in my Magic Markers for a Mac as I entered the design world. It would be thirteen years before I

O dry bones, hear the word of the Lord.

EZEKIEL 37:4 ESV

rediscovered lettering, the art of drawing letters. But God eventually brought me full circle, and it changed me from the inside out.

Dry Bones

My young-adult life was blessed. I was raised in the church under one of the most well-known pastors of our day. My childhood was full of sweet tea, sweet friends, and a close-knit family life. And as a firstborn, I was a rule-follower, always seeking to please and live up to the expectations of others. I became a born-again Christian at the age of eight, never had a rebellious phase, and never did anything that would bring shame to my family name. I was a good girl, and I knew it. Over time, my "good girl" status became more about me and less about God. I

began to take my salvation for granted. While I still had a desire for the Lord, I failed to see the evil in my heart and my deep, deep need for grace. My clean "good girl" life that was blessedly free from rebellion and bad influences meant, in my mind, that it didn't take as much grace to save me. What a powerful lie from the devil that was. I cringe at the thought now.

Because I took grace for granted, my heart slowly became colder and colder to the Word of God. I became critical and bitter. Though I was an adult, my childhood faith was still not yet my own. On the outside, I was attending church, singing in the choir, and playing the part of a good Christian woman. But inside, my heart was cold toward spiritual things.

In this dark period of seven years, God faithfully carried me through the profound grief of my mother's passing from cancer and the fearful unknowns of new motherhood when my son was born shortly thereafter. In the spiritual dryness of my heart, I prayed that God would help me feel something new toward Him. For all my churchgoing, I lacked spiritual depth, and I didn't know where to start.

God in His goodness used a friend to persuade me to join a Bible study with her. You see, God is continually drawing all people to Himself. He waits to be gracious to you. That Bible study was the very first time I opened God's Word on a daily basis and began to study it from front to back, start to finish. I began to read it with a heart to know God, not for a quick fix for my daily problems or as a thing to cross off my to-do list. God took my heart of stone and gave me a heart of flesh. It was the most amazing, exciting time of my walk with God.

But within weeks, I was confronted with spiritual warfare. I came face-to-face with a sinful temptation that dropped me to my knees. In that struggle, I began to see my true aptitude for sinfulness. I saw that I wasn't a good girl by my own doing. No, it was

I will give you a new heart and put a new spirit in you;

I will remove from you your heart of stone and give you a heart of flesh.

EZEKIEL 36:26 NIV

4

Christ in me that made me good. I finally saw the grace I'd long taken for granted as the great gift that it is.

When did we decide we were too grown up to be artists?

Can you relate to my story? Whether you grew up going to church or are just starting your spiritual walk with God, guard against spiritual apathy. When you realize the depth of your sinfulness and the measure of grace poured out on you, that is when you'll stop taking for granted the precious salvation God lovingly and freely gives. God's Word is life. The more you study it and saturate your heart in it, the more strength you'll have to resist the devil's flaming darts.

Faith and Lettering

I rediscovered my love of letters shortly after my spiritual reawakening. As my appreciation for God's Word grew into a deep love of truth, lettering became the way I could meditate on it—a way to make much of Him. King David wrote Psalm 51, in which he says, "Open my lips, Lord, and my mouth will declare your praise" (v. 15 NIV). My pen became my way of declaring the Lord's praise.

One day as I worked at my computer, I stumbled upon a hand-lettered piece of art. It was beautifully done, and I was immediately inspired to try the technique myself.

My first attempt was Exodus 14:14. I remember penciling and erasing, penciling and erasing. The slow process of drawing it and reading it to myself became a powerful tool for memorization. How exciting, that I could do something *fun* as a means of learning

The first thing we learn about God in the Bible is not that He is holy, loving, omnipotent, or omniscient. The first characteristic He reveals to us is that He is creative!

JORDAN RAYNOR, *Called to Create*

Scripture! Hand-lettering Bible verses became my outlet; it fed me creatively and spiritually. It wasn't long before I was lettering in my Bible, creating sketchnotes during sermons, and encouraging others to join me in the practice.

Rediscovering Your Creativity

I tell you my story because I hope it will resonate with you on a spiritual level as well as a creative level. Remember, when I rediscovered lettering, I had put away my pens and markers to pursue a career in graphic design. I thought playing with letters was a thing for kids.

Did you also enjoy being creative as a kid? Did you fill notebooks with your artwork and present them to your parents? Did you doodle on your class notes? Maybe

you picked up this book because you love expressing your creativity. Or perhaps, instead, you yearn to be creative. Maybe you often tell people, "Oh, I'm not creative, but I wish I was!"

Let me tell you something— You are a child of God. You were made in His image. And guess what? Our God is a creative God! He is the Creator, the ultimate Maker. So there is creativity in your DNA that you cannot deny.

This book will teach you that you can learn lettering. Yes, you. And you'll find that lettering is a powerful tool to grow your faith.

How to Use This Book

There are many ways to incorporate hand-lettering into your life, spiritually and practically. This book will show you how. Its purpose is to inspire you, to reignite your devotional time, to imprint Scripture upon your heart, and to help you dig deep into the Word of God through the art of lettering.

Faith and Lettering is designed for you to read from start to finish, because each chapter builds upon the last. It can also be a future resource for design inspiration, practice prompts, or reference. You'll learn the basics of hand-lettering, Bible journaling, sermon sketchnotes, and even creating encouragement cards for friends.

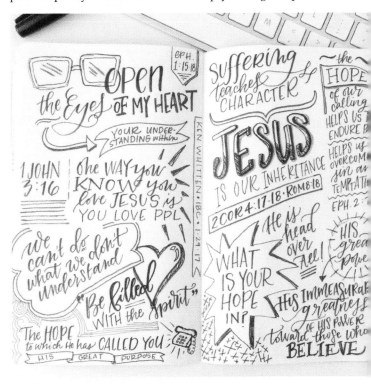

Something special happens when you slow down and take time to focus on Scripture in a creative way. God's Word does not return void, and anytime you're diligent about saturating your heart with biblical truth, our creative God will use it.

Let's rediscover our creative sides, our penchant for doodling. Let's "letter for the Lord" together.

Fix these words of mine in your hearts and minds.... Write them on the doorframes of your houses and on your gates.

DEUTERONOMY 11:18, 20 NIV

Section 1

Lettering Basics

Terms and Tools

Getting Started

*T*he first thing you should know about lettering is that all the supplies in the world cannot substitute for consistent time spent practicing. All you really need in order to learn lettering is a pencil and notebook paper. But if you're inclined to add some nice supplies to your toolbox, here is a list of my essentials.

Essential Tool Kit

1. **Pencil.** My favorite pencils are the **Blackwing** pencils because of their soft, buttery lead. These are premium pencils but amazing to sketch with. *Economy runner-up: mechanical pencils.*

2. **Fine-Line Pen.** You'll need some pens with fine tips to add small details to your lettering. The **Staedtler Pigment Liners** and **Sakura Micron Pens** are widely used. They have archival ink that is waterproof and fade-proof, so you can easily use watercolors with them. Best of all, they come in many different line widths. These are my go-to lettering pens.

3. **Brush-Pen.** A brush-pen is a calligraphic pen that gives thick or thin lines depending on the pressure you give it. The best brush-pens to start with when you're learning are the **Tombow Fudenosuke** hard tip and soft tip. If you'd like to add some color, try the **Pentel Touch** pen.

4. **Eraser.** With a quality pencil, you need an equally good eraser. The **Tombow Mono NP** eraser is my favorite, and I've tried a lot of erasers. It erases cleanly without any smudging or smearing. *Economy runner-up: PaperMate Pearl Eraser.*

5. **Ruler.** A ruler is a must for hand-lettering. Look for one around 6"–8" long.

6. Colored Pencils. My favorite colored pencils are the **Crayola Twistables**. They're easy to use, don't require sharpening, and are inexpensive. You may even have them already in your art supply stash.

7. Sketchbook. Paper is important. Look for a plain sketchbook that you don't mind messing up. If it's too pretty, you may feel intimidated and not want to use it. My favorite is a sketchbook with a spiral on top so that the spiral doesn't get in the way.

8. Notebook or Journal. Any high-quality notebook that's a good size for carrying around works. I keep a Moleskine Cahier by my Bible to use for creative sermon notes and a notebook at home for lettering special verses. Some have covers that are plain so you can customize them yourself. Others already have beautiful designs. There is a companion journal to this book that has lots of practice space, lies flat, and has more tips and practice prompts.

9. Bible. A Bible is a must for *Faith and Lettering*, but you don't have to buy a special Bible to write out Scripture. *Note: In the Bible Journaling section, I'll cover several different journaling Bibles.*

What Is Lettering?

Lettering is a fun and relaxing pastime. It's perfect for Scripture meditation and reflection.

Repeat after me: "Lettering isn't handwriting. Lettering is drawing shapes." Handwriting is quick—efficient. Lettering is slow—artistic. Many talented hand-letterers will tell you that their handwriting looks completely different and maybe not that great! But this fact that lettering is not handwriting is exactly why anyone can learn it! You just have to be willing to practice your shapes.

I know you want to start creating hand-lettered masterpieces right away, but it's important to first learn some terms you'll read throughout the book.

First, people frequently ask, "How do you learn to draw different fonts?" This is a distinction I want to help you with, so that you know what you're talking about and are more knowledgeable in it. Fonts and lettering are not the same thing, though people often interchange the terms. Let's take a look at what each one means.

the term
"**LETTERING**"
REFERS TO BOTH
Calligraphy
&
~HAND~
LETTERING

LETTERING: Lettering is simply "the art of making letters." It is any kind of letters made by hand, and this includes both calligraphy and hand-lettering.

CALLIGRAPHY: Calligraphy means "beautiful writing." While traditional calligraphy is all about uniformity, modern calligraphy is about finding your unique style. Though it's a *type* of penmanship, it's not handwriting, and it is usually done with a special pen.

HAND-LETTERING: Hand-lettering is drawing or illustrating letters like you would draw shapes. The letters themselves become art.

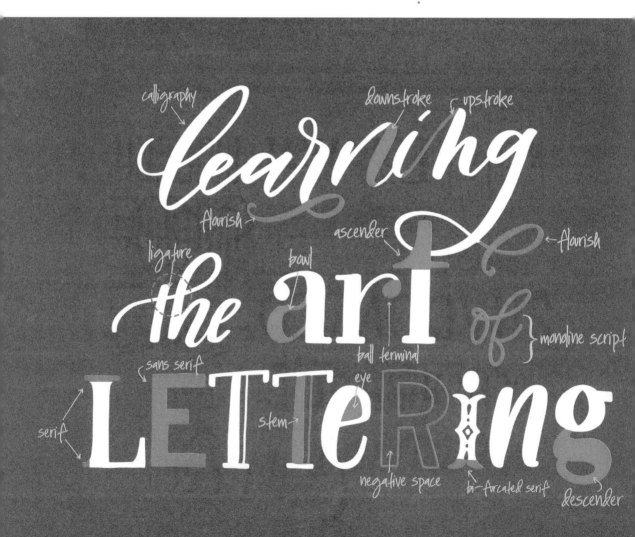

ascender line
cap-height
x-height
baseline
descender line

By contrast, **FONTS** are used on a computer for typesetting, traditionally in printed material. They're used in books, brochures, websites, and materials that contain a great deal of written copy. Fonts are helpful for learning different *styles* of hand-lettering, but fonts are not considered hand-lettering themselves.

Lettering has a lot of charm that computer fonts can't achieve. A font is the same every time you use it. Every Helvetica *E* looks the same as the last. But lettering is much more fluid and can bend to what the design calls for.

Terminology

Lettering Styles

Remember how I said that people mistakenly ask how to learn to draw other fonts? What they mean to ask is, How do you learn to draw other lettering styles? Lettering styles are endless, so once you learn the basics and know how to study letterforms, you can pick up any style you choose to learn. Lettering is simply building up a **memory bank** of what letters look like in different styles and then training your hand to draw them. It does take practice, but anyone can do it! **Remember: hand-lettering isn't handwriting! It is drawing shapes.**

Three Major Styles

There are three main lettering styles every hand-letterer should know: Serif, Sans Serif, and Script. These styles can be broken down into more subcategories, but these top three form the foundation for all letter styles. Learning them is the best way to jump-start your lettering skills, as you'll learn the specific forms of each letter and build a memory bank for each style.

SERIF: Serif letters are characterized by small strokes called serifs at the end of each horizontal and vertical stroke that makes up a letter. This style traditionally has varying thicknesses in the strokes and is considered easier to read. A serif font will be found mainly in books and the body text of printed pieces.

SERIF

ABCDEF
GHIJK
LMNOP
QRSTU
VWXYZ

SANS SERIF: Sans Serif letters are characterized by a uniform thickness and lack of serifs ("sans" means "without"). This is a more modern style, and a sans serif font is often found in website text because it's considered easier to read on a screen.

SANS SERIF

ABCDEF
GHIJK
LMNOP
QRSTU
VWXYZ

SCRIPT: Script letters are characterized by joined lowercase letters and can appear fancy, casual, whimsical, etc., depending on the specific style of the letterforms and flourishes.

Now that you have the introductory stuff down, you can get started on learning how to letter in the next chapter.

classic *bouncy*
Whimsical STREAMLINED
SHADOWED Fun
open *ribbon* AVANT GARDE
RoUGH Formal MODERN

Building Your Memory Bank

"How do I learn new styles?"
Notice the letters around you. Start paying attention to the special characteristics that distinguish a style or font. Here are some examples of things to look for:

1. Notice how the top bowl of the *B*s are slightly above the center line.

2. Notice whether the bowls are lined up or if one is bigger than the other.

3. Notice where and how the letter sits on the baseline.

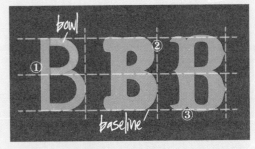

Now that you know what to look for, print out your favorite computer fonts in a large point size on a sheet of paper. Use tracing paper to copy the letters, paying attention to each letter's details. You'll learn what makes that font unique and how to mimic it in your lettering. Don't worry about perfection. Just learn the essence of the style.

ABCDEFG
LMNOP
UVVW
AaBb Cc Dd
Mm Nn Oo Pp Q
Ww Xx Yy Zz 1234

Aa Bb Cc Dd
Gg Hh Ii Jj Kk
Ll Mm Nn Oo Pp
Qg Rr Ss Tt Uu
Vv Ww Xx Yy Zz

1234567890

Let's Start Lettering

Overview

Before you can start lettering like a pro, you need to learn basic letterforms—letter by letter, then word by word. This chapter will show you how to draw the three basic styles and how to teach yourself any style you want to learn. So put away all your fancy tools and grab a trusty old pencil for these exercises.

Uppercase versus Lowercase

If you study the hand-lettered art around you, you'll notice that letters are regularly drawn in uppercase. Lowercase letters make an appearance every so often, but they're typically not used with much frequency. Why is that? The various ascenders and descenders in lowercase letters are the culprit. These competing negative and positive shapes make it much more difficult to compose a tight, aesthetically pleasing art piece when a great number of lowercase letterforms are used.

Funny, though, how the opposite is true for script styles, where uppercase letters don't look well side by side. The fluidity of script allows the letters to move around each other much more easily, even with competing ascenders and descenders. If you're drawing a script style, you'll want to keep uppercase letters at a minimum and focus on the lowercase.

For that reason, we're going to focus our attention on learning the case that's most relevant for each style.

Hand-lettering is building a letter step-by-step. You start with the basic skeletal form, then add the weight to the bones, and then finish off the details of the style and fill it in. Let's see how that looks for our main three styles: serif, sans serif, and script.

Serif

Sans Serif

Script

Staying Anchored

C, G, O, V

Letters with curves on the bottom tend to look smaller, which gives the illusion that they're hovering above the baseline. To fix that, let the letter come slightly below the baseline to "anchor" it.

Similarly, with the letter V, the sharp point at the bottom can look like it's floating, unanchored. Let it dip below the baseline.

A A A A A A A A

B B B B B B B B

C C C C C C C C

D D D D D D D D

E E E E E E E E

F F F F F F F F

G G G G G G G G

H H H H H H H H

I I I I I I I I

23

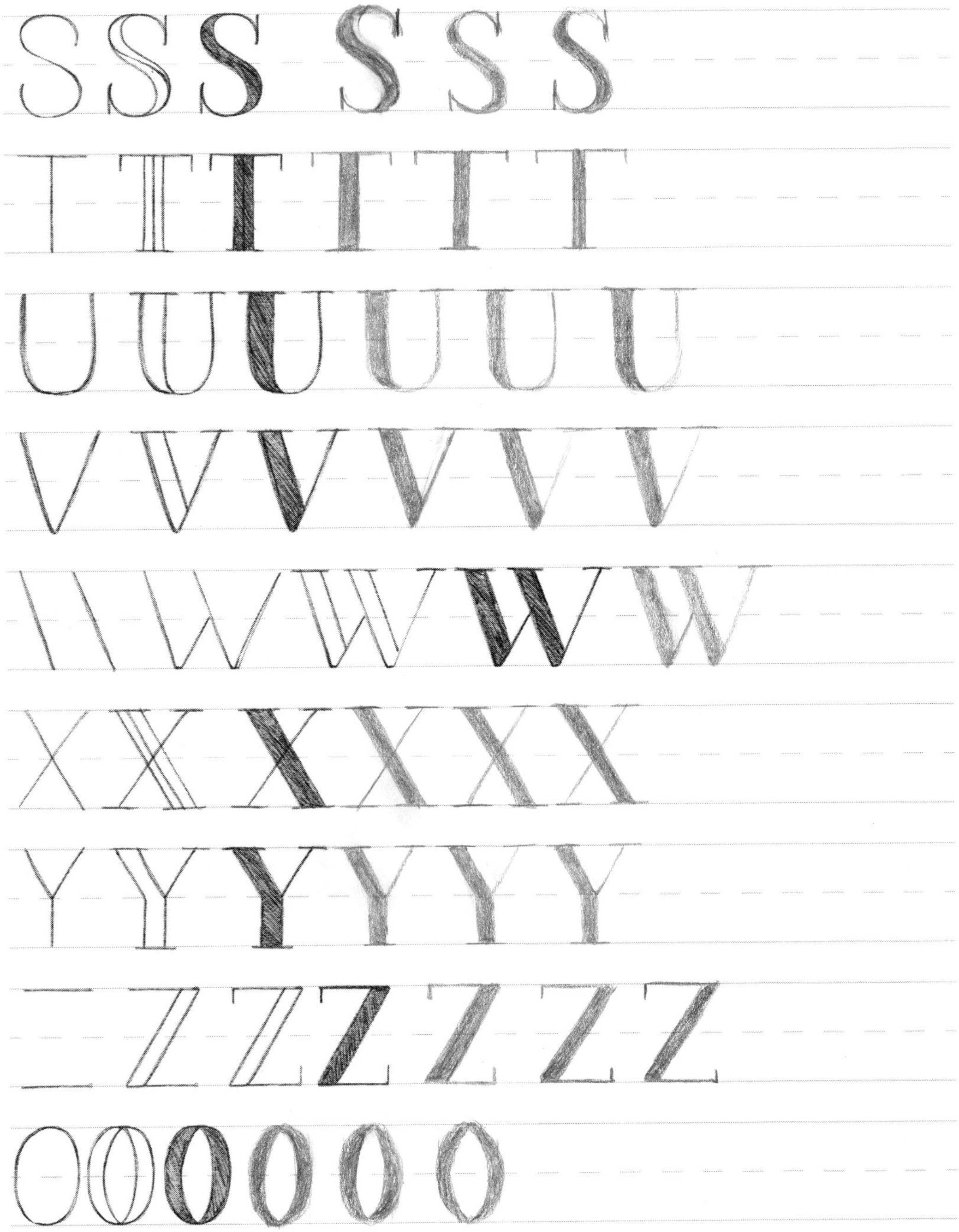

SSS SSS

TTTTTTT

UUUUUUU

VVVVVVV

WWWWWWW

XXXXXXX

YYYYYYY

ZZZZZZZ

OOOOOOO

1 1 1 1 1 1 1

2 2 2 2 2 2 2

3 3 3 3

4 4 4 4

5 5 5

6 6 6

7 7 7

8 8 8

9 9 9

Serif Variations

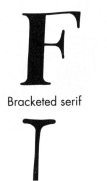

Bracketed serif

Slab serif

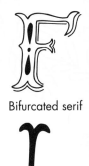

Bifurcated serif

Letter Notes

—*W* is not an upside-down *M*.

—*N*'s thick downstroke is in the middle, not on the outsides.

—For a *T*, set the width of the arm first, so you know how wide the letter is going to be.

Sans Serif

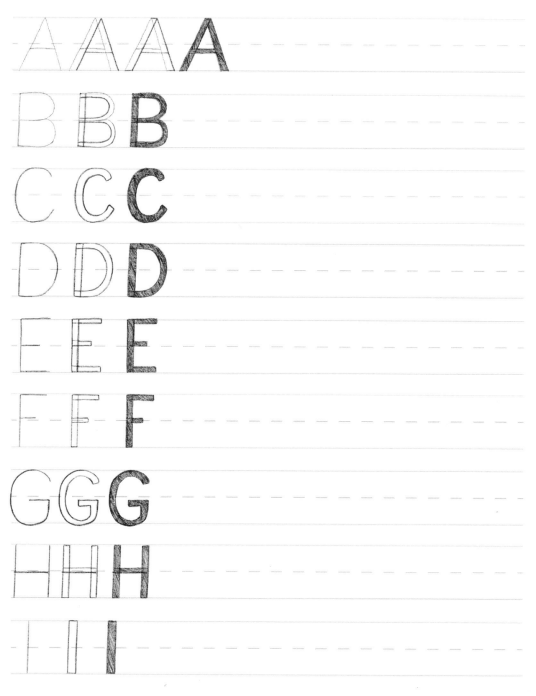

JJJ**J**

KKK**K**

LLL**L**

MMMM**M**

NNNN**N**

OOO**O**

PPP**P**

QQQ**Q**

RRR**R**

29

1 1 1

2 2 2

3 3 3

4 4 4

5 5 5

6 6 6

7 7 7

8 8 8

9 9 9

Sans Serif Variations

Skinny

Modern

Cartoon

Thin Those Horizontals

A, H, B, T, L: Horizontal lines tend to look fatter, so make them slightly thinner. It will trick your eyes into thinking they're the same width as the vertical lines.

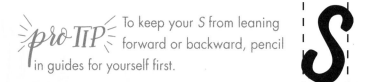 *pro-TIP* To keep your *S* from leaning forward or backward, pencil in guides for yourself first.

A Note About Script

A script style with a basic single line is called a **monoline.** Script with an added thick downstroke is often called faux calligraphy, or **fauxligraphy**. Faux calligraphy is not a "lesser" version of calligraphy. On the contrary, it opens the door to even more fun techniques *and* it's useful for lettering on surfaces like chalkboards, glass windows, mirrors, or any other special surfaces you might want to decorate.

To hand-letter a script style, start with the monoline, add a thick downstroke, and then fill in the downstroke.

Script

a a *a*

b b *b*

c c *c*

d d *d*

e e *e*

f f *f*

g g *g*

h h *h*

i i i

j j j j

k k k k

l l l l

m m m m

n n n n

o o o o

p p p p

q q q q

r r r r

$\mathcal{S} \mathcal{S} \mathcal{S}$

$t\, t\, t$

$u\, u\, u\, u$

$v\, v\, v$

$w\, w\, w\, w$

$x\, x\, x$

$y\, y\, y\, y$

$z\, z\, z\, z$

Script Variations

Curvy ribbon

Classical

Whimsical

pro TIP

For consistency in a piece,
make your downstrokes the
same thickness for each letter.

Curvy Problems

One common mistake with faux calligraphy is making
a curved downstroke too heavy on the bottom or top.
Look at the examples to see how to taper for a more
visually appealing downstroke.

The Look-and-Learn Method

Do you want to learn a new style of lettering? Lettering styles are endless. You're limited only by your **imagination.**

Here's my most effective way to teach yourself *any* style you can imagine:

1. Print off a full alphabet of your favorite font.

2. Cover the alphabet page with tracing paper or marker paper (I prefer marker paper), or use a light box if you have one. You want to be able to see the printout underneath.

3. Draw guides for your baseline and cap height.

4. Trace each letter carefully. You may want to fill up a page practicing that one letter over and over. Pay attention to where it's thick or thin, where the crossbars are, and what makes it unique as you learn the intricacies of the style. This not only builds your memory bank— it also builds muscle memory!

5. Now draw another set of guides. This time, using the traced letters as a reference, draw the basic skeleton of each letter.

6. Then fill out the details of the letters, watching for overall thickness and size. Try to match the shapes as best you can. You'll see that mine above isn't a perfect replica. I need some more practice! The more you practice, the better you'll get!

7. Once you're happy with your letterform, render it out with a pen.

8. Then erase the pencil marks.

Creating Your Own Unique Style

There's only one sure way to get good at lettering and creating your own unique style. You have to do a lot of lettering. You have to do a lot of practice. Practice often, and practice a lot!

I want to share some encouragement from Ira Glass, a well-known radio host who gave a talk on doing creative work. In the beginning, he says, there's a gap between what you want to do and what you have the ability to do. You know what you want it to be and you have good taste, but you simply can't achieve it yet. Your work is disappointing to you. And that's where most people give up. But this is normal to all creatives. You have to push through it. "It is only by going through a volume of work that you will close that gap and your work will be as good as your ambitions."

Tips to Get Started

1. Draw each letter fifty different ways. Draw everything you can think of, no matter how basic or elaborate. Over time, you'll identify what feels natural to you and what is pleasing to your eyes.

2. Be inspired by other artists, but don't copy. Instead of trying to make your work look exactly like someone's you admire, identify what you like about it and try it yourself. Maybe you like one artist's R and another artist's S. Figure out a way to take another artist's ideas to come up with your own.

3. Create first. Sure, you can use social media platforms for inspiration—in fact, I encourage it! But rather than look at other artists' work before creating your own, try creating FIRST. You'll be fresher and less likely to fall into comparison traps or feel discouraged when yours doesn't look the same as what inspired you in the first place.

4. Practice fifteen minutes every day. If you struggle with practicing, set a deadline for yourself to practice a little every day. Write it in your planner, put it on your schedule, and make a date with yourself and your pencil. You'll be so glad you did!

A good hand-letterer will have a working knowledge of each style. It takes time and practice to build your memory bank, but with each style you learn, your skills and technique will improve!

ABCDEFG
JKLMNO
STUVW

abcdefg
mnopqr
uvwxyz

1234567890

Modern Calligraphy

The Basics of Brush Lettering

*T*he three styles you learned previously are all types of hand-lettering. You drew shapes and added weight and details to them to change the basic look of each letterform. Now we're switching gears to talk about **modern calligraphy**, which is a type of *penmanship*—writing letters versus drawing letters. If that makes you nervous because you struggle with your handwriting, be assured that calligraphy is also very different from your natural handwriting. I'll never forget where I was or how I felt when I watched that first video of a calligrapher doing her thing. It was mesmerizing and beautiful.

Modern versus Traditional

Traditional calligraphy is a formal, precise art. Each style has specific rules regarding slants, shadings, and shapes for calligraphers to follow. It can take years to master. As much as I love it, I don't have the patience or the time to cultivate that level of precision. Fortunately, there's been a rise in popularity of *modern calligraphy*, which has looser rules and gives the freedom to develop a personal style. This is the style I'll be teaching you.

It's important to remember that even though the rules are more fluid, lettering is meant to convey a message to your audience, so readability is key.

Don't get so loose on your letter formations that people have trouble distinguishing your letters.

43

Calligraphy requires some special tools to achieve the beautiful thick and thin lines you're probably accustomed to seeing. Where traditional calligraphy is done with a penholder and nib that are dipped into ink, modern calligraphy can be done with either a dipped pen or a brush-pen. **The brush-pen is my best friend.**

Brush-pens have a flexible tip and are capable of producing a thicker line when pushed down with pressure. Using one feels unnatural at first. In fact, when I first picked up one, I hated it! It took me many, many tries to begin to feel comfortable using it. So be sure to manage your expectations the first time you use one (meaning, don't expect to immediately start writing sentences and selling art online).

The best way to remember what should be thick or thin is to remember that every time your pen goes down, your line should be thick. Hold your pen at a 45-degree angle and lightly move the tip upward to create a thin **upstroke**. Apply pressure by pushing down as you move the pen down to create a thick **downstroke**.

upstroke

no pressure

versus   pressure

downstroke

Learning the Strokes

Opposite of the cursive learned in school, where we're taught to string every letter together without picking up the pen, calligraphy is a series of separate strokes put together. *Picking up the pen is key to getting a good letterform!*

The other key to good letterforms is to learn the basic strokes. Calligraphy drills are the best place to start. I have pages and pages of these drills in my notebook. They are a smart way to get comfortable with the motions and build memory muscle.

upstrokes

downstrokes

ovals

entrance strokes

underturns

overturns

compound curves

ascending loops

descending loops

Calligraphy uses these basic strokes to make up each letter. Let's break that down and see how each letter is formed.

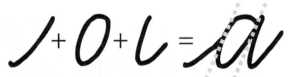

Entrance stroke, main stroke, exit stroke

Look at each letter and practice forming these letters on your own. Don't forget to pick up your pen between each stroke!

pro TIP Keep your calligraphy on a straight baseline while you're learning, to keep your letters from getting distorted!

Check Your Slant

Slant is the angle at which your letter sits. Some styles are perfectly straight, whereas other styles are heavily angled. Your slant is important to maintain. Pencil in angled guides to help you keep consistency. You can also test your slant by placing pencil guides on top of your lettering *after* you practice.

Start with guides to keep your slant consistent.

lazy

Test your slant with penciled guides to see how you did.

oblivious

ɿ·o·ɩ	*a*	**a**	*a*	*a*
ℓ·ə	*b*	**b**	*b*	*b*
ɿ·c	*c*	**c**	*c*	*c*
ɿ·o·ℓ	*d*	**d**	*d*	*d*
ɿ·e	*e*	**e**	*e*	*e*
ɿ·ƒ·ɿ	*ƒ*	**ƒ**	*ƒ*	*ƒ*
ɿ·o·ɉ	*g*	**g**	*g*	*g*
ɿ·ℓ·ɿ·n	*h*	**h**	*h*	*h*
ɿ·i	*i*	**i**	*i*	*i*

a

b

c

d

e

f

g

h

i

ı + j   *j*   *j*   *j*   *j*

ı + ı + k   *k*   *k*   *k*   *k*

ı + l   *l*   *l*   *l*   *l*

ı + ı + n   *m*   *m*   *m*   *m*

ı + n   *n*   *n*   *n*   *n*

o   *o*   *o*   *o*   *o*

ı + l + o   *p*   *p*   *p*   *p*

ı + o + f   *q*   *q*   *q*   *q*

ı + r   *r*   *r*   *r*   *r*

j

k

l

m

n

o

p

q

r

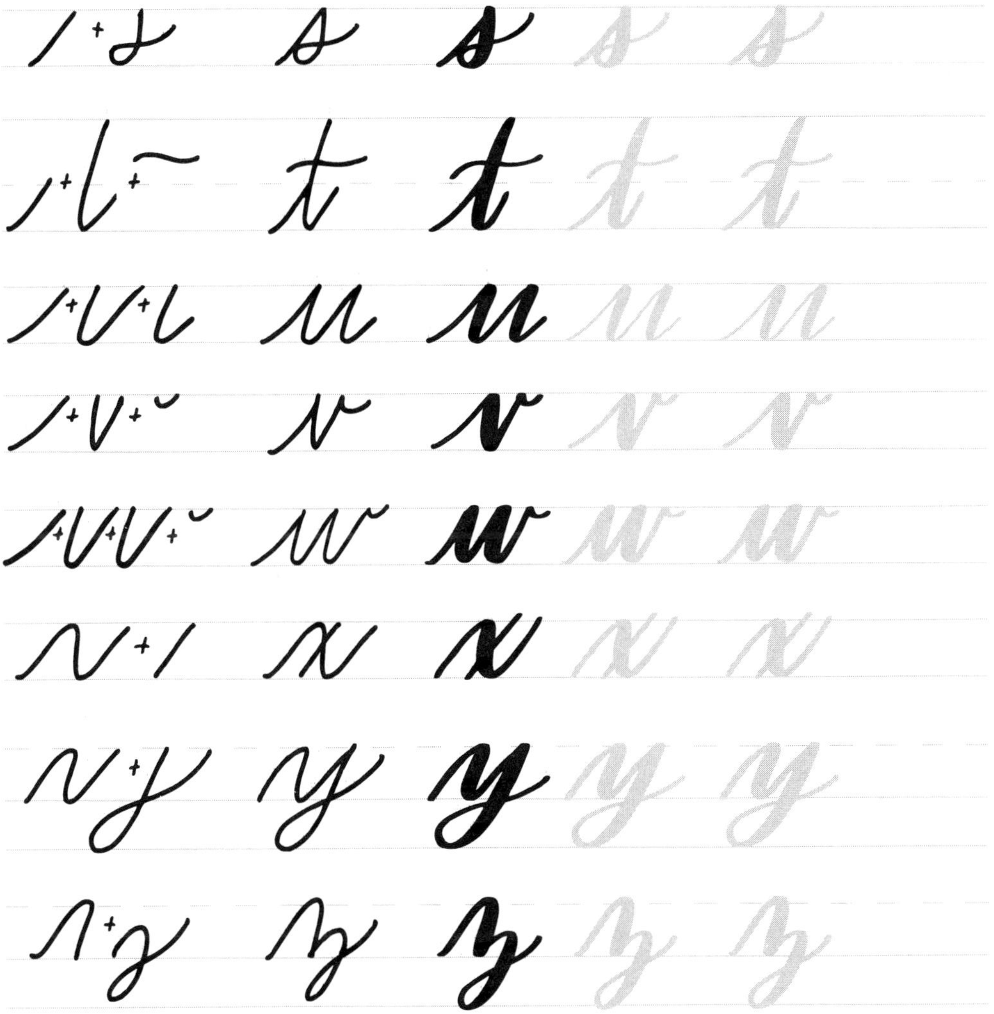

s

t

u

v

w

x

y

z

0 1 2 3 4 5

6 7 8 9

A B C D E E
variation

F G G H I J
variation

K L L M N O

P Q Q R S T

U U V W W W
variation

X Y Y Y Z Z
variation   variation

53

practice Practice drawing the capital letters on page 53.

From Letters to Words

Let's go back to grade school for a minute and reflect. Do you remember learning cursive? You may not—maybe you blocked it out!—but I'll bet your teacher made you write your letters over and over and over. I'm watching my son do it now. He has his little practice sheets, and sometimes he "letters" with me. He often peers over my shoulder and asks, "How do you get your letters so perfect?" And I tell him, "There's no such thing as perfect, but practice will make you better and better!"

Now I'll tell you the same thing: **There's no such thing as perfect, but practice will make you better and better!** So once you're comfortable making letters, you're ready to advance to connecting them and making words. With letter connections, everything depends on the exit strokes.

Most letters connect with an exit stroke at the baseline.

a c h l

Other letters connect with an exit stroke at the midline, or **x-height**.

o v w

The exit stroke of one letter will affect how it connects to the next letter.

Still others connect as they come out of a loop.

g j q y

The exit stroke of one letter will become the entrance stroke of the next letter. Therefore, the exit stroke of one letter affects how it connects to the letter after it. Always be aware of what your *next* letter is, and think ahead about how they need to connect.

Common Connections

er re st es ie gr el

in ye at ve sh

Trace these words, which include many different letter combinations.

graduation

jukebox

shepherd

freedom

smile

hallelujah

happy

zealous

expression

Dancing Baseline

You're building your skills one step at a time! Once you're comfortable writing words on a straight baseline, you can practice a **dancing baseline**. This is one of my favorite things about modern calligraphy because a dancing, or moving, baseline brings a beautiful, interesting appeal to lettering.

The biggest thing to remember is balance. An imaginary line drawn through the middle of the word shouldn't tilt sharply one way or another, downward or upward (unless it's intended to be at an angle!).

Moving Baseline : An unpredictable, invisible line used in modern calligraphy to exaggerate some letters and give a dancing or bouncing effect to words.

Note that just because a letter *could be* exaggerated doesn't mean it *should be* exaggerated. If every letter is emphasized, the word will end up looking stretched or skewed. A good rule of thumb is to exaggerate every other or every third letter.

Below are letters with arrows showing the direction of where the exaggeration would go. If one letter dips down, the next letter should be placed slightly higher or evenly to that imaginary baseline, alternating the dips and bounces so the word ends up looking balanced.

upward

straight

wrong

You don't want your *N* to dip down so low.
It looks distorted, and it's right next to the *G* descender.

abcdefghijkl
mnopqrstu
vwxyz

hello

faith

love

pray

friend

trust

good

letter

Caution: Step back and look at the letters to make sure the exaggeration isn't distorting them. An *a* shouldn't look like a *q*, an *E* shouldn't look like an *L*. In fact, *a*, *c*, and *e* should never be exaggerated in a dancing baseline.

Getting Rid of the Shakes

I have shaky-hand syndrome. Even with lots of practice, my calligraphy especially is prone to wobbles. It's okay. There are plenty of reasons for this.

If you're sure you aren't jittery from too much caffeine, here are some things you can do to defeat the shakes:

1. Warm up. If you haven't done any writing today, your muscles are cold. Do some drills—upstrokes, downstrokes, ovals, etc. Practice your ABCs or write a favorite verse to get your blood flowing and your muscles warm.

2. Use a pencil and practice. Sometimes we're shaky because we're nervous. The permanence of using pen can intimidate you, even if you don't realize it. Use a pencil and ease those nervous tendencies.

3. Breathe out. If you're practicing calligraphy, those thin upstrokes are really hard to do and require a lot of muscle control. So breathe **in** on a downstroke and **out** on an upstroke. Sounds silly, but try it.

practice Give it a try. Use a pencil so you can focus on the dancing baseline and not about where the thick strokes should go. This technique is called "dancing" because there is some rhythm associated with it. Your muscles will build up this rhythm as you practice. Have fun with it!

Section 2

Creative Elements

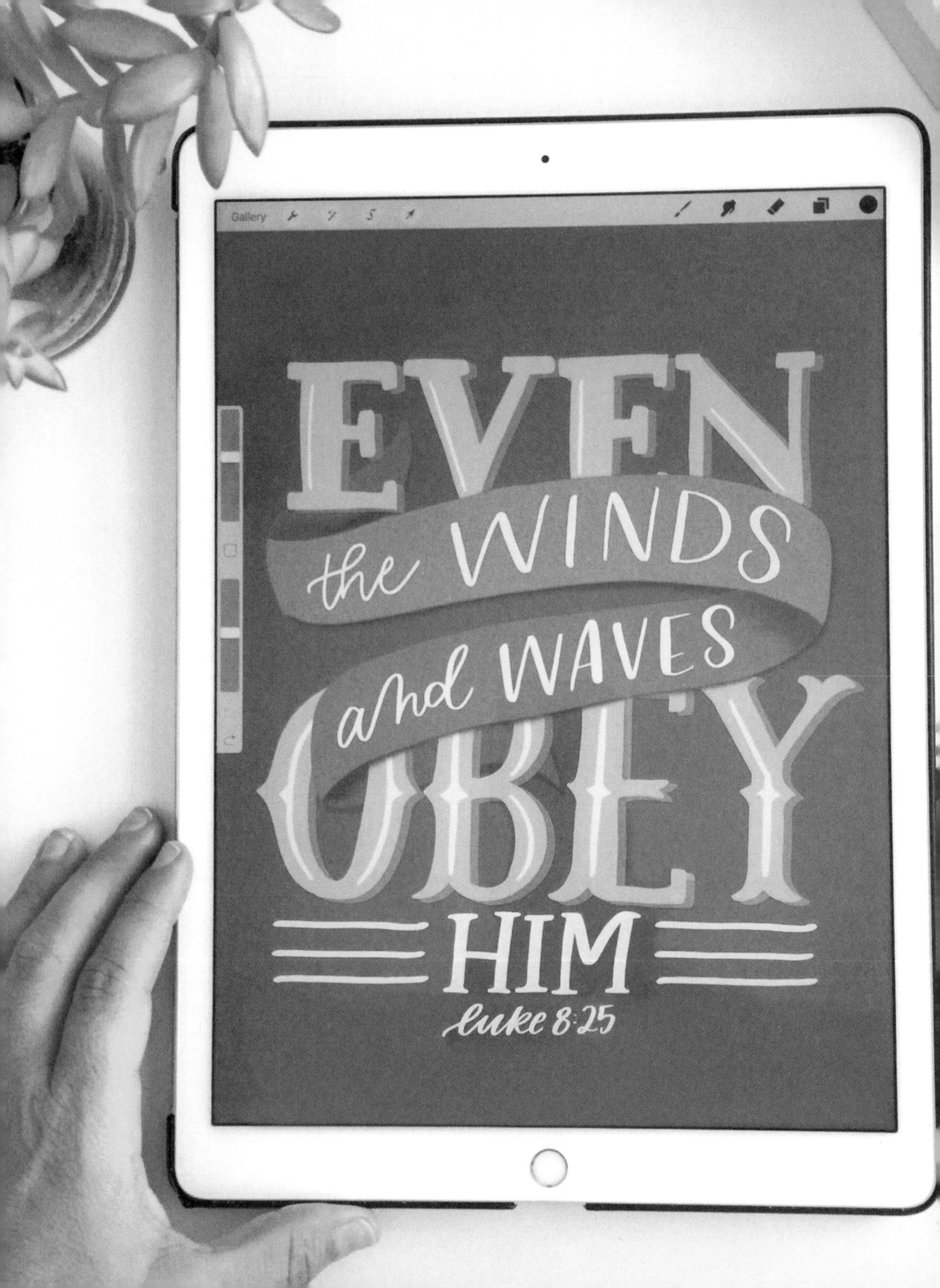
Gallery
EVEN
the WINDS
and WAVES
OBEY
HIM
luke 8:25

Ribbon Banners

Easy Step-by-Step Instructions for Drawing Five Styles of Banners

Once you understand how to draw letters and you want to start lettering phrases, the next step is to add some banners to your skills.

Banners are a fantastic way to enhance lettering layouts. They look impressive and difficult to draw, but the good news is, they're easy when broken down step-by-step. You can use banners in many different ways, from highlighting important words in an art print to containing titles in creative sermon notes.

Once you learn these basic banners, you can create your own combinations or variations with flair. As with anything, the more you draw ribbon banners, the better you'll get. Follow along with me in these easy step-by-step instructions.

1. Straight Banner

Straight banners are simple to draw, but they tend to look best with precise lines. Feel free to use a ruler to make your banner straight and balanced.

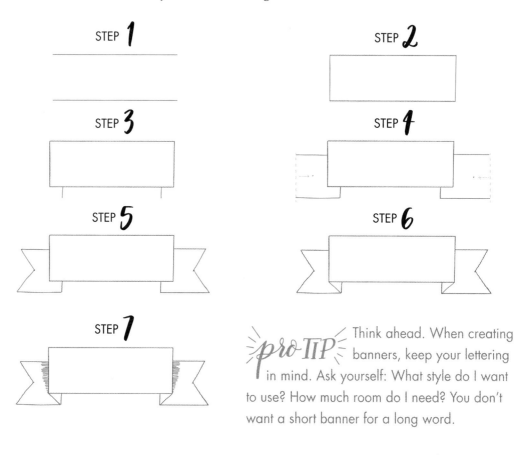

STEP 1

STEP 2

STEP 3

STEP 4

STEP 5

STEP 6

STEP 7

pro-TIP Think ahead. When creating banners, keep your lettering in mind. Ask yourself: What style do I want to use? How much room do I need? You don't want a short banner for a long word.

practice Draw a straight banner and letter your name inside.

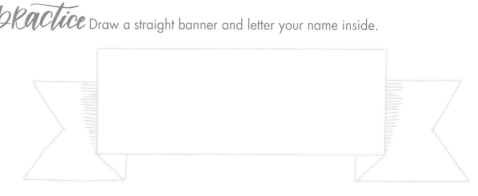

2. Wavy Banner

Wavy banners are a bit easier to draw than straight banners because you don't have to be as precise with them. They look a little more complicated to create, but follow along and you'll master them in no time.

STEP 1

STEP 2

STEP 3

STEP 4

STEP 5

STEP 6

STEP 7

pRActice Draw a wavy banner and letter the word "Grace" inside.

3. Double Banner

Double banners look great with short phrases in them. Keep in mind that both sections should be the same width.

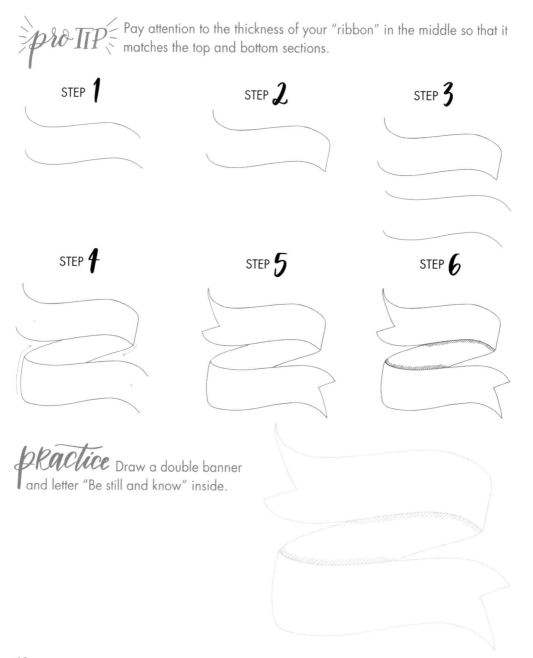

pro TIP — Pay attention to the thickness of your "ribbon" in the middle so that it matches the top and bottom sections.

STEP 1

STEP 2

STEP 3

STEP 4

STEP 5

STEP 6

pRactice Draw a double banner and letter "Be still and know" inside.

4. Trailing Ribbon

A trailing ribbon is a more elaborate take on the wavy banner—the more curves, the better. Once you get the hang of it, go ahead and add as many curves as you want!

 *pro TIP* With curvy banners, curving the corner edges will help your banner look more realistic.

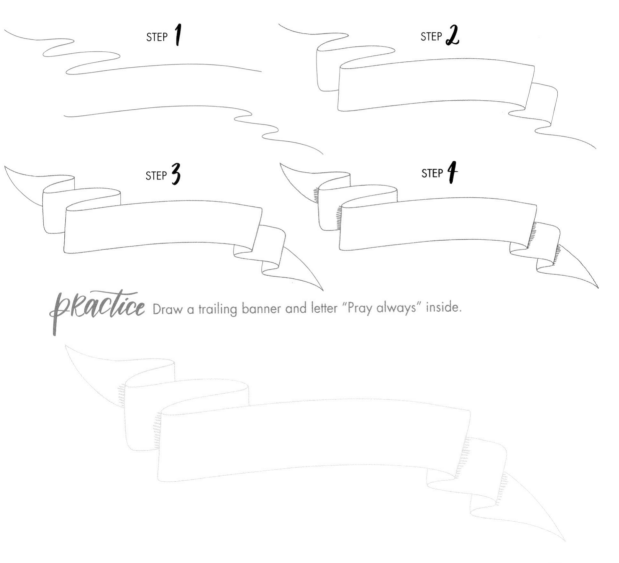

STEP **1**

STEP **2**

STEP **3**

STEP **4**

pRActice Draw a trailing banner and letter "Pray always" inside.

5. Scroll

Scroll banners are containers that can be utilized in a range of ways. Use them in creative church notes to hold large quotes, titles, or lists. They can be vertical or horizontal, and they immediately draw the eye because they're so decorative and impressive-looking.

pro TIP

Curve your corners slightly instead of making sharp, defined corners by starting at the backward *S* and continuing out the line horizontally.

STEP **1**

STEP **2**

STEP **3**

STEP **4**

STEP **5**

practice Draw a scroll and letter the phrase "It is well with my soul."

As I mentioned at the start, there are many, many variations that can be made to these basic banner and ribbon designs. Play around with them on your own and see what you can come up with!

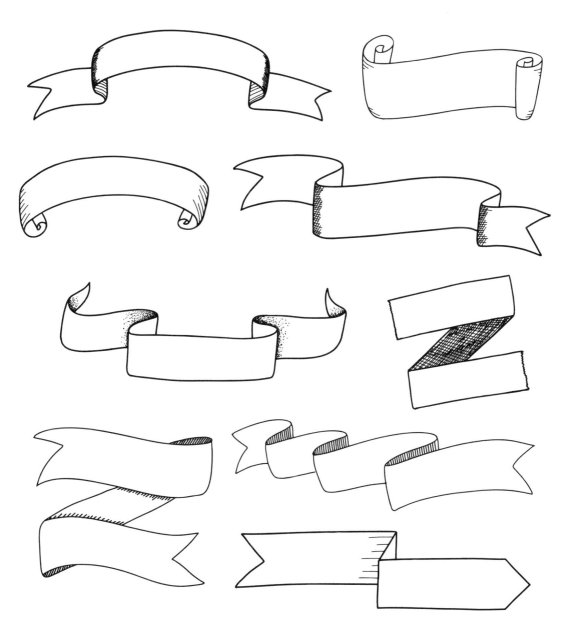

The Lord is near to the brokenhearted

— psalm 34:18

Flowers

Easy Step-by-Step Instructions for Drawing Five Different Flowers

Flower Examples Used in Lettering

Drawing was never something I considered myself to be good at, but once I started looking closer and breaking objects down into shapes, it became much easier to try new things. Flowers can appear hard to draw, but the beautiful thing about art and nature is that there is a lot of fluidity. You don't have to recreate the exact shape to mimic the right look.

Here are some of my favorite flowers and the step-by-step instructions to draw them. Try these out with a pencil and have fun!

1. Open Rose

Roses are elegant and timeless, and these roses are easy to draw by simply building up petals, layer by layer. You can choose to make them full or sparse depending on how closely you place the petals and how many layers you add.

STEP 1   STEP 2   STEP 3

STEP 4   STEP 5   STEP 6

practice Hand-letter your name and embellish it with a rose at the end.

2. Daisy

Daisies are friendly, casual flowers, and this style is also simple to draw. The hardest part can be making sure the petals are evenly spaced, which is why I start off by drawing the petals directly opposite each other. Once the first petals are placed, it's easy to fill in the rest of the flower.

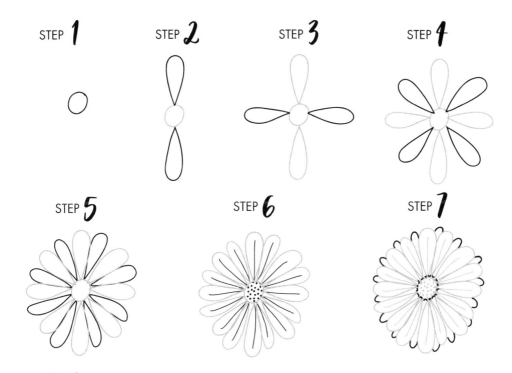

practice Hand-letter "Do not be anxious about tomorrow" and add some trailing daisies underneath.

3. Tulip

Tulips are casual, charming flowers in bright colors. I find tulips look best drawn with a stem. Put two or three together in a bunch for a great look.

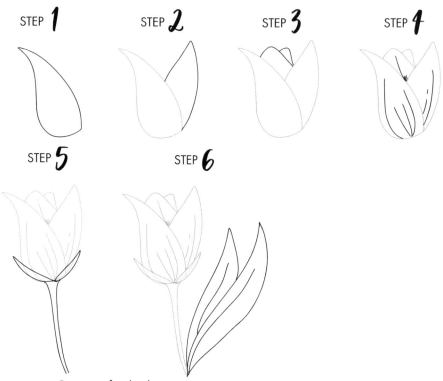

STEP 1 STEP 2 STEP 3 STEP 4

STEP 5 STEP 6

Once you finish inking your stem,
erase the overlap on the bottom of the tulip.

4. Poppy

Poppies are a vibrant scarlet-red color, often used to symbolize peace or eternal sleep. They make a big impact when drawn in clusters.

5. Peony

Peonies are feminine, delicate flowers with giant blooms in pinks, whites, and yellows. This is the most advanced flower we have to draw, but I'm confident you can do it.

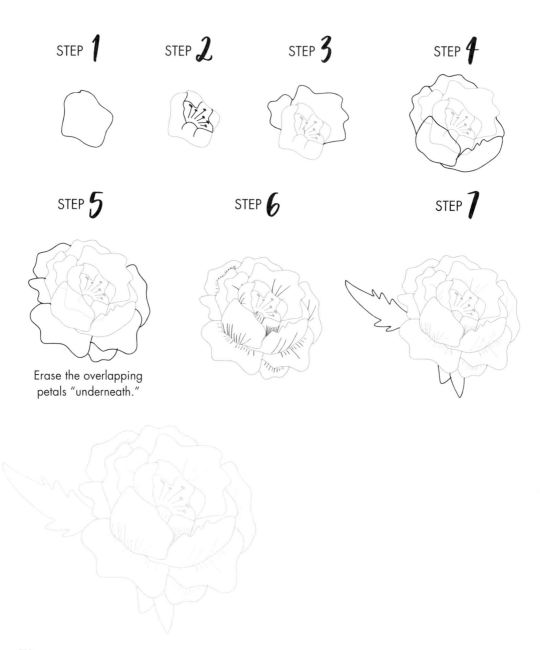

STEP 1

STEP 2

STEP 3

STEP 4

STEP 5

Erase the overlapping petals "underneath."

STEP 6

STEP 7

practice Draw a bouquet using three of the flower types you've learned.

Wreaths

Easy Step-by-Step Instructions for Drawing Five Styles of Wreaths

A wreath is a beautiful way to pull florals and lettering together to make a cohesive design. In this chapter, I'll show you how to draw five different wreath styles to get your creativity flowing. Use these wreaths as a jumping-off point to create your own amazing art.

1. Laurel Wreath

Classic and simple-looking, a laurel wreath is an easy addition to any lettering phrase. The key to a laurel wreath like this one is to make the leaves larger at the bottom and smaller at the top, keeping an equal number of leaves on both sides.

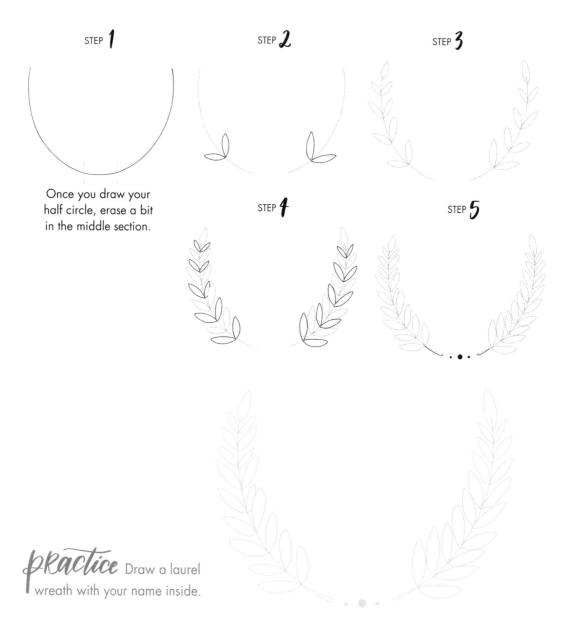

STEP 1

Once you draw your half circle, erase a bit in the middle section.

STEP 2

STEP 3

STEP 4

STEP 5

pRactice Draw a laurel wreath with your name inside.

2. Minimal Wreath

With a minimal-style wreath, your lettering can be the star. Start with a few interlocking, imperfect circles and add leaves all the way around.

STEP 1

STEP 2

STEP 3

STEP 4

practice Draw a minimal wreath and hand-letter "Seize the day" inside.

3. Magnolia Wreath

A magnolia-leaf wreath has a classic, Southern charm. You can add a simple monogram inside or hand-letter a short phrase. Start with a circle and begin layering leaves around the shape. A magnolia wreath usually has a heavily layered look where the leaves lie on top of one another.

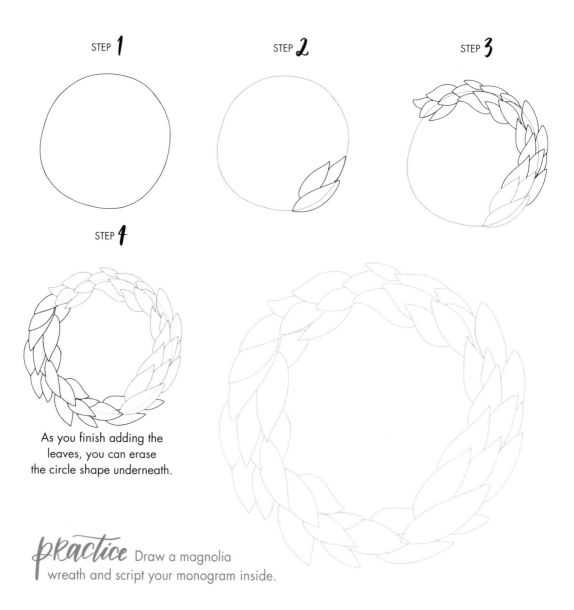

STEP 1

STEP 2

STEP 3

STEP 4

As you finish adding the leaves, you can erase the circle shape underneath.

practice Draw a magnolia wreath and script your monogram inside.

4. Christmas Wreath

This Christmas wreath combines a mix of evergreen and holly. You can add more stems and leaves to thicken it up or do fewer stems to make it sparser.

STEP 1

STEP 2

STEP 3

STEP 4

practice Draw your Christmas wreath and write "Christ is born" inside.

5. Floral Wreath

The floral wreath incorporates several different botanical elements. For floral wreaths, start with the rule of thirds, which will help you focus on balance versus symmetry. Draw three of each element, spread out around the wreath. If your wreath starts out with this balance, it will look more interesting than if it is perfectly symmetrical. If your wreath has holes in the last step, you can fill it in where it's needed.

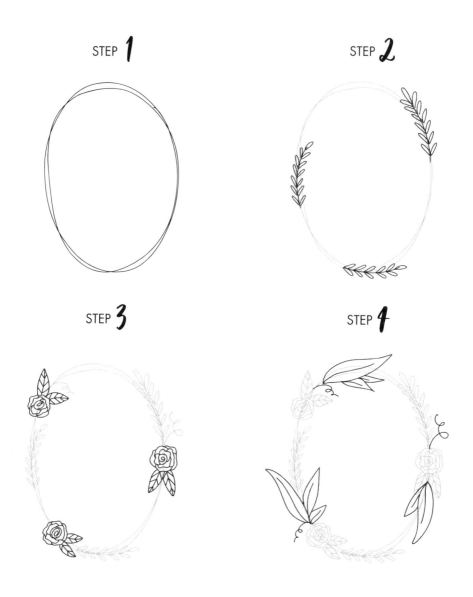

practice Draw your floral wreath
and hand-letter "Pray big" inside it.

Flourishes and Frames

Further Embellishment for Your Lettering

*F*lourishes and frames are our last element to learning hand-lettering. A flourish adds a dramatic or elegant flair to your lettering, whereas a frame adds detail and a distinctive look to polish off your piece.

Flourishes can be added to existing designs to fill space or added to letters to give them prominence. But they are also great for covering mistakes, changes, or additions to existing letters or words. It is spiritually symbolic to turn those mistakes into something beautiful. Once you learn the technique, adding a flourish to smear, ink drop, or other "oops" becomes part of a unique design. Just like God uses our mistakes and sinfulness for a greater purpose, we can use little mistakes to pull together a meaningful, unique design.

Flourishes

practice

practice

Ligatures: Flourishes can connect two letters.

 Write your name with flourishes.

Letter "The Day of the Lord" using ligatures and flourishes.

O vs. *O*

practice

Frames

1. Wooden Frame

1. Draw an outer square that is big enough to encompass your lettering.

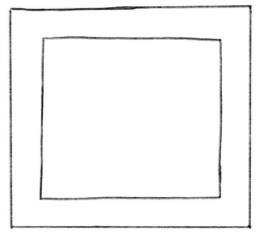

2. Draw a smaller square inside with equal thickness on all sides.

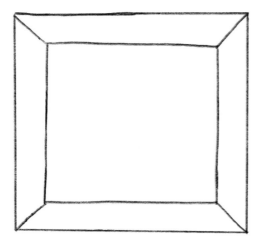

3. Attach the two shapes at each corner.

4. Add in some lines for the wood grain and knots on all sides.

2. Ornate Frame

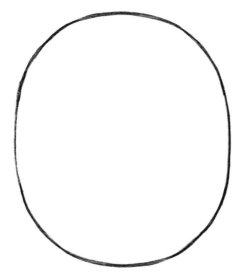

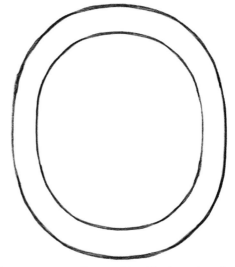

1. Draw an oval that is big enough to hold your lettering.

2. Draw a smaller oval inside, keeping the same thickness all the way around.

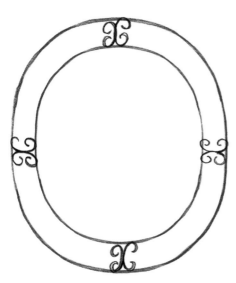

3. Add four flourish shapes on all four sides.

4. Add flourishes inside each quadrant.

3. Flourish Frame

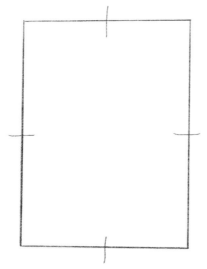

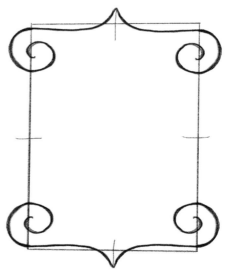

1. Lightly pencil a rectangle and mark the middle points.

2. Draw flourishes on the top and bottom that peak in the middle.

3. Fill out the flourishes with some added embellishment.

4. Connect the top and bottom flourishes with straight lines. Erase the original marks.

4. Double-Line Frame

1. Lightly pencil a square with small half circles in each corner.

2. Erase the corners.

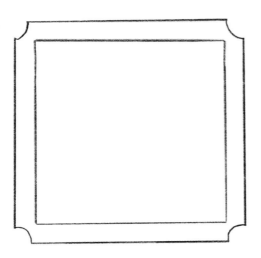

3. Draw a smaller square inside the first one.

4. Add an extra line detail to the inside square and a flourish on each corner.

5. Swirly Frame

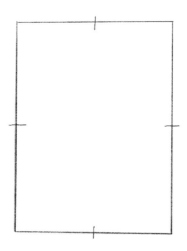

1. Lightly pencil a rectangle and mark the middle points.

2. Draw flourishes on the top and bottom with opposite curves. Try to make each side match as much as possible.

3. Connect the top and bottom flourishes on each side. Again, try to make the left side proportional to the right.

4. Make small tick marks in each corner. Erase the original rectangle.

For from Him & THROUGH HIM and TO HIM are ALL things. To Him BE the Glory FOREVER AMEN!

IF WE ASK anything ACCORDING to His will HE HEARS US 1 JOHN 5:14

Section 3

Layout and Technique

Putting It All Together

How to Create Beautiful Layouts

I'm often asked, "How do you mix different lettering styles?" and "How do you come up with your layouts?" These questions refer to the art of composition, one of the most important parts of design. You can create beautiful flowers and banners and lettering all day, but knowing how to pull those elements together into a well-planned layout is where the magic happens.

It's an exciting challenge to decide where to place each element so they fit together in an aesthetically pleasing way. This may sound intimidating, and you may be tempted to skip to the next chapter—but don't. You've already learned the basic key elements you'll need. Now let's learn some ways to put them together.

Like anything, crafting good layouts takes practice, but eventually ideas will come more naturally to you! *This chapter is a step in moving past the beginner stages to the next level.*

Composition: the placement or arrangement of visual elements or ingredients in a work of art.

105

The Five Cs of Composition

Here are five approaches you can take to develop your layout. You don't have to use all five in one layout, but they *can* be mixed and matched. Don't be afraid to try different things to see what works best.

Word Count: Ideally aim to keep your phrase at ten words or less. The more words, the more cumbersome the layout becomes.

Practice Prompts

1. Love one another
2. God is love
3. He makes all things new
4. He makes me brave
5. You are the light of the world
6. He is above all things
7. The Lord is near
8. One God, one Lord, one faith
9. Here I am; send me
10. The righteous will live by faith
11. He is the Alpha and the Omega
12. Teach us to number our days
13. From his fulness we have grace upon grace
14. Create in me a clean heart, O God
15. Grow in grace and knowledge of the Lord Jesus Christ

1. Combine. Use more than one lettering style in a piece. Remember the three basic styles: serif, sans serif, and script. Combine them to add interest; two to three styles should do.

2. Contrast. Mix it up with thick and thin styles, small and large words, curvy flourishes and stick-straight letters. Use contrast to emphasize certain words. Check out the contrasts in the example below:

3. Contain. Fit words in containers like banners or shapes. Use lines and frames to create boundaries, emphasize, or decorate.

Your Turn! Using the Practice Prompts sidebar practice lettering a word or phrase on your own.

4. Contour. Similar to the containers, you can utilize curves, diagonals, and arches to change up the direction of your words and make your design more interesting. Notice in the example that the words "Give Me Jesus" are curved instead of straight.

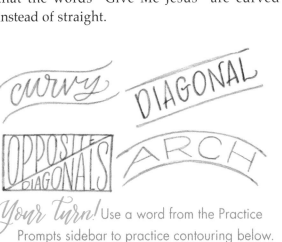

Your turn! Use a word from the Practice Prompts sidebar to practice contouring below.

5. Construct. Build each word to fit nicely together, like puzzle pieces. Instead of placing everything on a straight baseline, look for ways to create movement or bounce—and avoid large areas of "trapped" white space. This will produce a nice cohesive look.

Start by drawing your main word of emphasis and build around it.

In this example, notice how the words fit tightly together without glaring gaps in the composition.

Here's an example of what this looks like both with and without the Construct principle.

First, notice the trapped white space in version 2, which is not ideal. Second, while the straight baselines in version 2 don't look bad, the overall layout lacks the unity and cohesion of version 1.

Make It Interesting!

Add details like drop shadows, in-lines, drop-lines, outlines, shading, 3-D, and stippling.

• Drop shadows (lines behind the letter)

 • In-lines (decoration inside the letter)

 • Drop-lines (shadow lines to one side of each stroke)

 • Outlines (tracing around a letter)

 • Shading (adding darker colors for dimension)

 • 3-D (filled-in drop shadows with a darker color)

 • Stippling (use dots to fill in the negative space to create a gradient)

For a change, use negative space inside letters to create detail. Dashes, dots, chevrons, stripes, color blending—there are many fun things you can do!

pro-TIP Repeat certain aspects of your design—style, thickness, size, etc.—to give it a unified look.

Check your layout for readability!

Make sure it follows the normal reading pattern: left to right, top to bottom. Keep that natural flow. Strive for a cohesive look. You want a stranger to be able to read it easily.

Lettering in a Shape

It's a fun challenge to letter inside a shape, the words filling the space but still being legible. Here are some examples of lettering in a shape. Use dashes or flourishes or squiggles to fill in the gaps in the shape as needed!

Try lettering inside these shapes as a good practice exercise.

Mason Jar

Prompt: The Lord bless you and keep you.

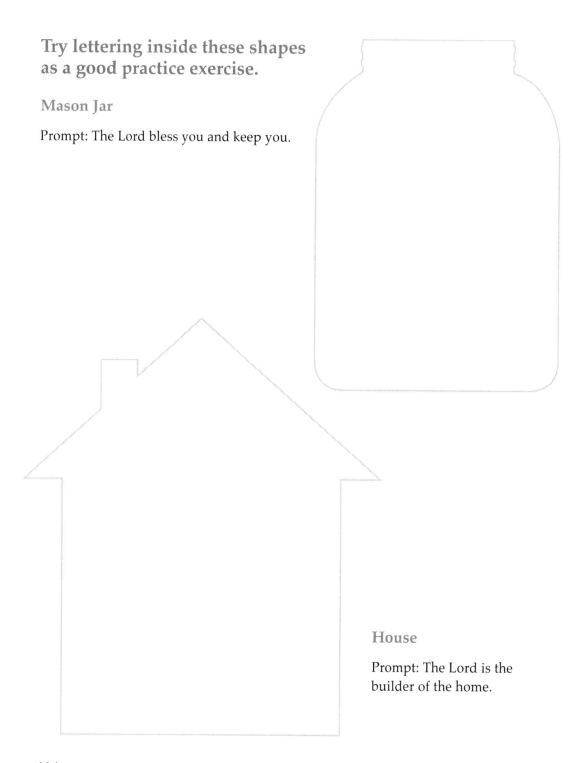

House

Prompt: The Lord is the builder of the home.

Heart

Prompt: Love the Lord with all your heart.

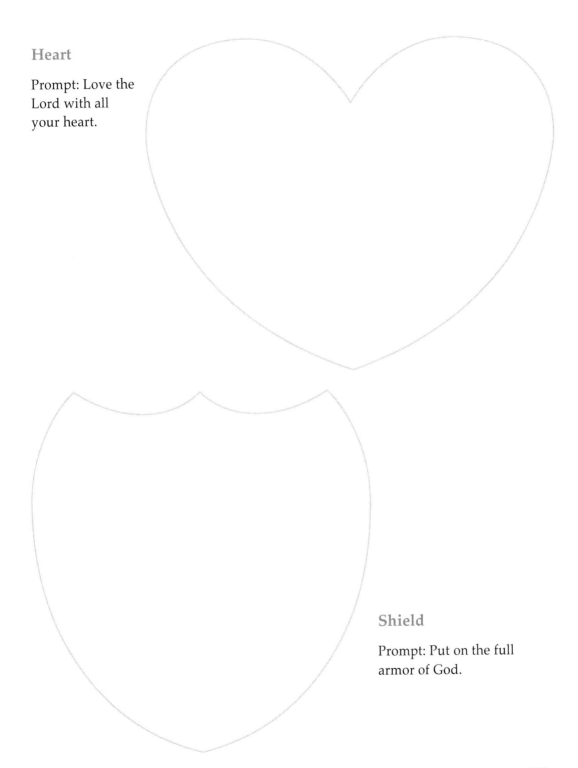

Shield

Prompt: Put on the full armor of God.

Just Start

Overcoming the Fear of the Blank Page

Creative Block

I know what it's like. You're excited to start, but when you first open your fresh sketchbook or brand-new journaling Bible, you blank out. You don't want to mess it up. You can't think of anything to draw. The feeling is intense. So you close your book and you think, "Maybe later."

The lack of creativity you feel when you stare at a blank page is nothing new. It's not unique to you. Writers feel blocked; painters lack inspiration. That blank page turns your brain to mush.

I have a background in graphic design, and I felt that same intimidation factor every time I created a new document. I was all ready to go—pumped up by starting a new project. And then I would stare at my screen. I'd get lost in the blankness of it. Thankfully, my creative director came to my rescue and encouraged me to follow a few brainstorming steps to get my creative juices flowing. And you know what? It always helped.

The creative process is like spinning a flywheel . . . an old, very heavy wheel that can only be moved by heavy pushing. It takes a lot of work to get it to move, but once it gets going, the *momentum* takes off and keeps it spinning! I love this illustration because it's true of your creative mind. **Creativity thrives with momentum.** Once you get going, you soar! It feels amazing. But the beginning is hard, and it can feel like a lot of effort going nowhere.

In this chapter I'll show you a brainstorming process to push past the fear of the blank page and get your creative flywheel spinning! Use the prompts in this chapter to practice.

Brainstorming Process

Start with a verse in mind. Check the list of prompts in the sidebar on page 123 if you're stuck.

1. **Write the verse.** Write down the verse on a scratch piece of paper. Nothing fancy here. If the verse is long, see if you can paraphrase it and make it shorter. Remember, five to ten words is preferable. (See page 150 for more on this.)

2. **Identify key words.** Circle the words you want to stand out.

3. **Make a list.** List everything you can think of that relates to the key words you circled—objects, feelings, places, adjectives . . . For example, if your verse talks about "light," you could write *light bulb, sun, rays, bright, lamp, lantern, yellow, glowing, hot,* etc. Some verses are more abstract than others, but this step is helpful if you're having a serious case of blank-page phobia.

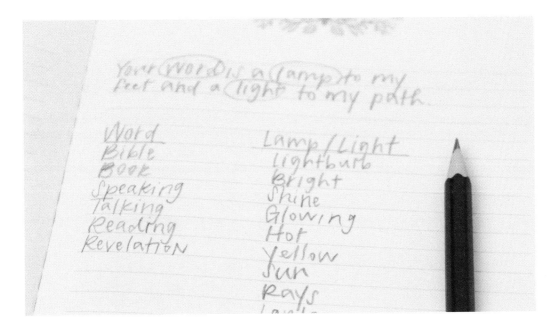

4. Draw two to three thumbnail sketches of possible layouts. Don't spend a lot of time here. Don't let yourself get bogged down. Don't even erase! Thumbnails are just little pictures that allow you to try out some ideas without fully committing or spending much time on them.

Memorization Tip:

Every time you write a verse, you are actively engaging your memory capacity.

The Drawing Process

Choose the thumbnail you want to develop. You may see things in each that you want to incorporate. This is where the process gets fun!

1. Draw your guides. On a fresh piece of paper, pencil some guidelines for where you want to place your artwork. I start with a rectangle box, usually 5 x 7 inches. (If you start too big, the size will be overwhelming. If too small, you won't be able to add much detail.)

Then lightly pencil in baselines and ascender lines (see pages 14–15) so you know where to draw your letters. Eyeball it.

Remember,

a pencil is your best friend!

Don't start with a pen.

2. Add the words. Once you have your lines set up, start lightly penciling in your words, *lightly* being the optimal word here. Draw. Erase. Draw. Erase. I do a whole lot of erasing!

3. Darken the pencil lines. Once you're happy with the placement of your words, go back over them to darken the pencil lines. You can make some refinements to the layout as you go.

4. Ink it. Use your preferred pens to ink the drawing on a fresh piece of paper. You can use tracing paper, graphite paper, a light pad, or whatever allows you to transfer the penciled sketch underneath. Go slowly and keep your hand as steady as possible.

Funny note: When I first started hand-lettering, I taped my sketches to a window and used the natural lighting to trace them. That was hard on my arms! But you do what you have to do.

pro TIP Keep a small sheet of paper under your hand as you work, to cover up the words you've already inked. This will keep them from smudging. I'm looking at you, fellow lefties!

You now have a finished design! You can frame it, turn it into a card, tape it into the binding of your Bible . . . or take a picture, scan it into your computer, and send it to a friend. Be creative and use your imagination! Your options are unlimited.

The more you do this process, the less daunting the blank page will feel. As with everything, practice is the key! As a creative person, you'll have days where you feel more inspired and adventurous than others. Don't let the struggles discourage you. This process works to push you past that "creative block" that afflicts all of us. So take the creative momentum you now have and do another one.

pro·TIP Want to frame your finished piece? First think ahead about what size or orientation it needs to be. A vertical versus a horizontal frame can make all the difference. Size the design to fit easily in a standard-size frame, and make it a quarter-inch smaller on all sides so the frame doesn't cut it off.

If you're stuck on what kind of lettering style to draw, play around with your word in different styles.

Lettering Prompts

1. Amazing grace, how sweet the sound!

2. Be still and know that I am God.

3. Great is His faithfulness.

4. It is well with my soul.

5. Give us this day our daily bread.

6. Bless the Lord, O my soul.

7. This is the day the Lord has made!

8. Fear of the Lord is the beginning of wisdom.

9. He will guard you in all your ways.

10. If God is for us, who can be against us?

11. Jesus is the Way, the Truth, and the Life.

12. God is our refuge and strength.

13. Blessed is the one who makes the Lord her trust.

14. He put a new song in my heart.

15. O taste and see that the Lord is good.

16. My soul makes its boast in the Lord.

17. The Lord is my shepherd.

18. You make known to me the path of life.

19. I will dwell in the house of the Lord forever!

20. The Lord will accomplish what concerns me.

21. Let the redeemed of the Lord say so!

Section 4

Faith Journaling

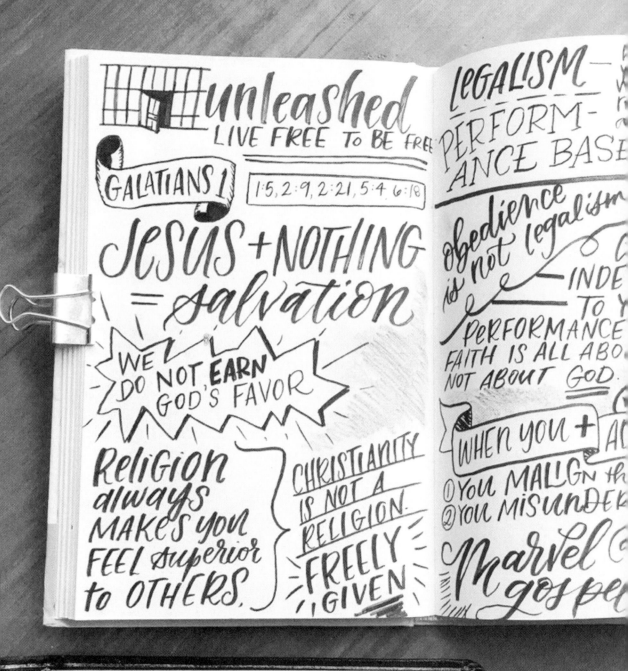

unleashed
LIVE FREE TO BE FREE

GALATIANS 1 — 1:5, 2:9, 2:21, 5:4, 6:18

JESUS + NOTHING = salvation

WE DO NOT **EARN** GOD'S FAVOR

Religion always makes you FEEL superior to OTHERS.

CHRISTIANITY IS NOT A RELIGION. FREELY GIVEN

legalism — PERFORMANCE BASE

obedience is not legalism

INDE TO Y
PERFORMANCE
FAITH IS ALL ABO
NOT ABOUT GOD.

WHEN YOU + A
① YOU MALIGN th
② YOU MISUNDER

Marvel @ gospe

1:15
Acts 9:15; Gal 2:9;
Acts 9:20; Matt
16:17

1:17
Acts 9:19-22

1:19
Matt 12:46; Acts
12:17

1:20
Rom 9:1; 2 Cor
1:23; 11:31

1:21
Acts 9:30; 15:23, 41

16 to reveal His Son in me so that I might preach Him among the Gentiles, I did not immediately consult with flesh and blood,

17 nor did I go up to Jerusalem to those who were apostles before me; but I went away to Arabia, and returned once more to Damascus.

18 Then three years later I went up to Jerusalem to become acquainted with Cephas, and stayed with him fifteen days.

19 But I did not see any other of the apostles except James, the Lord's brother.

20 (Now in what I am writing to you, I assure you before God that I am not lying.)

21 Then I went into the regions of Syria and Cilicia.

22 I was *still* unknown by sight to the churches of Judea which were in Christ;

23 but only, they kept hearing, "He who once persecuted us is now preaching the faith

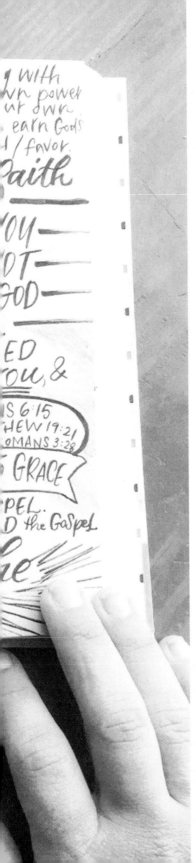

Creative Sermon Notes

*O*n the past, you could find me at church with note-book and colorful gel pen in hand, hunched over my Bible, writing perfectly outlined notes. I've always been an avid notetaker, all the way back to high school. If I didn't have a pen in my hand, I couldn't pay attention. But even when I took regular notes, my mind wandered easily. I would wonder what we were having for lunch or mentally make grocery-store lists.

Not anymore.

This chapter is probably my favorite one, because creative sermon notes, or sketchnotes, have been such a life-changing discovery in my life.

The term "sketchnote" was first coined by designer and author Mike Rohde, who wrote two books on the subject. Sketchnotes are simply visual notes that are taken live during a speech, a class, or, in this case, a church service.

When I started taking creative sermon notes, the mental grocery lists and daydreaming were no longer struggles.

Suddenly I was fully engaged in the message, listening intently, so I could visually convey the main ideas of the sermon in my notebook.

Just as hand-lettering Scripture is a powerful way to draw near to God and pursue a deeper faith, creative sermon notes can help you remember what a message was about even days later! It makes listening in church *fun*! In the

past, I would forget the point of the sermon by the time I got in the car to go home. I'm ashamed to admit that, being married to a pastor's kid and all.

The difference between regular note-taking and creative sketchnotes is this: You're not just passively writing word for word what you hear. Instead, your brain is actively working, processing what's being said, so you can write or draw the *main ideas* in a visual manner.

Now instead of throwing a used sermon notebook in a box (never to be looked at again), I enjoy rereading past sermon notes and remembering the great truths.

What does it take to be a sketchnote-taker?

A pen, *some* paper, *and a good dose of* imperfection!

How can creative sermon notes help you? The process is fun, you'll pay better attention, and you'll remember more from sermons than you ever did before.

Sketchnotes are not a new thing. Maybe you doodle in school and you're always getting into trouble for it. (Now you can tell your teacher that sketchnotes help you learn better!) Or maybe you look at this and feel terrified. Overwhelmed. You think, "I could never do that." It's time to change your mind-set, friend.

There are no hard-and-fast rules to creative note-taking. There's really no right or wrong way to do it, either. And, guess what, you will make mistakes. You will misspell words. Everyone does. It's okay!

So, relax, take a deep breath, and repeat after me: "I can do this!"

If you did an Internet search for "sketchnotes," you'd find a variety of different ways people implement it. You'll have your own style too, once you get started. Some

people are proficient illustrators and use a lot of images in their sketchnotes. Others rely on just two or three lettering styles and simple elements to complete their sketchnotes. As always, this is something that you get better at in time! Remember, you can do this!

Tools

Keeping it simple, all you need is a pen and paper. I keep a calligraphy brush-pen and a regular gel pen with my Bible, as well as a small Moleskine cahier. I like these notebooks because they're lightweight, they lay flat (that's important), and the size is perfect for filling up two pages with sermon notes. Moleskine paper tends to be hard on brush-pens, so you may want to look for another option if that's a concern for you. The Leuchtturm1917 notebooks have smoother paper and are of nice quality.

pro-TIP Keep scratch paper next to you to quickly jot down something you don't want to forget but can't get to yet.

Elements of Creative Sermon Notes

The challenge with creative note-taking is that the message is different every time. There aren't any hard-and-fast rules, and you never know what you're going to end up with on paper. But the creative challenge is part of the fun and beauty of it, and ultimately, it'll enhance your skills and make you better.

Tips for Successful Sermon Sketchnotes:

 Focus. Sit somewhere you're not easily distracted (the way you are next to that friend who's always whispering to you), and pick a spot with good lighting if you can.

 Listen. Process what you hear, but don't try to write down every word the speaker says. Just record the main ideas or what stands out to you.

 Write. Write quickly and legibly. Concentrate on getting the words down, not on drawing elaborate letters. You can always go back and embellish. Feel free to use abbreviations.

 Draw. Think of visual elements you can incorporate. Don't get bogged down here. It shouldn't distract you from listening. Leave a space to come back to and draw it later if that helps.

First things first: manage your expectations. Chances are, the first few times you create sketchnotes will feel a little awkward. You might not be happy with the outcome. You might have trouble keeping up or knowing where to put certain points. Congratulations! You're completely normal. No skill comes easily the first time you do it. At the end of this chapter, we'll talk about what to do when you make mistakes. But for now, keep in mind that you must go through some awkward stages creatively before you can produce masterpieces.

Creative sermon notes are more than simply writing words in different styles of lettering. I'm going to teach you some simple elements that, when combined, work together to give you a nice, full layout that's interesting and fun to look at.

Remember, it's more important to get down the main points of the message than get bogged down in elaborate lettering techniques.

1. Lettering Styles

Sketchnotes are different from the hand-lettering we've talked about previously. Hand-lettering is slow-paced and letters are developed bit by bit, often with pencil first. In contrast, sketchnotes are done quickly, and you don't have much time to think or plan because you don't know what's coming next. So because of that, you should know your lettering strengths. If you're new to lettering and you don't move quickly, don't try to draw lettering styles that are hard for you. Develop two to three styles you can do quickly. Focus on that first.

If you're more advanced and can sketch bubble letters or Victorian letters with your eyes closed, go for it! *Remember, it's more important to get down the main points of the message than get bogged down in elaborate lettering techniques.*

Here are the main lettering styles I usually incorporate. You can see that they're pretty simple. And they are the same styles as we discussed earlier, the "big three," just simplified. Their look changes depending on which pen you use.

ABCDEFGHIJKLM
NOPQRSTUVWXYZ

ABCDEFGHIJKLM
NOPQRSTUVWXYZ

ABCDEFGHIJKLM
NOPQRSTUVWXYZ

ABCDEFGHIJKLM
NOPQRSTUVWXYZ

abcdefghijklm
nopqrstuvwxyz

abcdefghijklm
nopqrstuvwxyz

Using a fine-line pen, gel pen,
or fine-tipped marker

Using a calligraphic brush-pen

You can certainly embellish your lettering if there's a lull in the message or after it's over. Here are some simple examples for embellishing your lettering:

1. Thicken your letters by adding weight to them.

ABCDEFGHIJKLM
NOPQRSTUVWXYZ

2. Add a drop line.

ABCDEFGHIJKLM
NOPQRSTUVWXYZ

3. Create negative space with faux calligraphy or by turning your sans serif lettering into serif lettering. (Note that this requires some planning ahead because extra spacing is needed between the letters.)

abcd ABCD ABCD

4. Add in-line detail to negative space.

abcd ABCD ABCD

Adding Variety and Contrast to Lettering

Back on page 107, you learned how to mix and match styles for contrast. Those same principles apply for creative sermon notes. Here are some ways you can give your compositions variety.

2. Containers

Containers are visually appealing and serve to separate different points while keeping your notes organized. Here are some examples:

3. Dividers/Lines

Dividers are similar to containers in that they visually separate main points or ideas. Use these dividing lines between subpoints, in lists, or to add emphasis. Here are some basic dividers you can use:

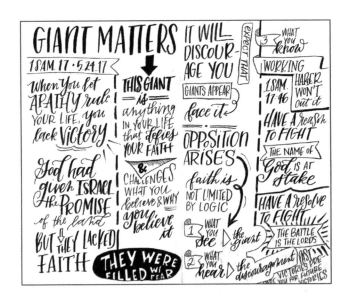

4. Arrows

Arrows will direct your eyes from one point to another. If you want to show a progression of thought, use arrows to connect one container to another.

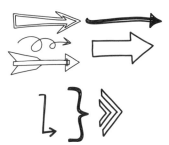

5. Common Doodles

Doodles will pack a big punch when you scatter them throughout your notes. Chances are you already know how to doodle some simple things. You can build up a mental database of objects that you know how to draw without much effort.

You may even want to bring a pencil into the service with you to quickly sketch out ideas. Don't be afraid to try new things. This is how you stretch your skills and grow.

If you're not sure how to draw something or you're not able to listen at the same time, you can leave a little space for it and add it later.

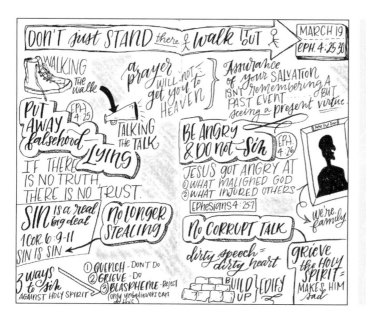

Information to Include in Your Notes

- Date
- Speaker
- Location
- Sermon Title
- Main Scripture Passages
- Main Ideas

practice

6. Filler Ideas

I like to see a full page when I'm done, but that doesn't always happen. It depends on the sermon and how quickly I worked. If I have room to fill, I'll do several different things:

Big space to fill: write out a Scripture passage used in the sermon.

Space around the edges: use shadowing, hashes, dots, or flourishes

How to Practice

I know this may be overwhelming at first. Remind yourself, "I can do this." You don't have to use *all* of these elements every single time. But familiarizing yourself with sketchnote elements will make you feel more confident because you'll have the tools in your mental toolbox ready to go. Start practicing at church. I get to practice once or twice a week, and it's great to do it on the fly.

For additional practice, take notes while listening to a podcast or webinar in the comfort of your home.

What to Do When You Make Mistakes

Be realistic with yourself. You *will* make mistakes. It's definitely going to happen, so just expect it. You don't have to rip out your page and start over. Keep cool, and keep going. Perfection is not the goal here, and most likely you're not selling your work, so it's okay.

Even so, our glaring mistakes have a way of eating away at us, so if you can fix it, great. Here are some ways to handle mistakes:

- **Turn it into a doodle.** A misplaced word can become a flower. An incorrect reference can become a heart. Or an arrow. Be creative and don't let it get you down.

- **Use the "squeeze" method.** If you miss a letter in a word, squeeze it in as best as possible. If you miss a word in a phrase, draw a little caret and write the word above it.

- **Use correction tape.** Correction tape is better than correction fluid because it's in a dispenser and can easily be carried in your purse. It's not wet, so there's no waiting for it to dry.

- When all else fails, **draw a line through it and write it again.** If you've hopelessly misspelled a word, just leave it. Chances are, you'll forget about it.

Bible Journaling

Creating Art in Your Bible

I discovered Bible journaling late one night as I scrolled through social media posts, searching for hand-lettering accounts to follow. This was shortly after I decided to throw my creative efforts into learning hand-lettering, and I was hungry for new techniques, tips, or inspiration. When I saw a Bible page illustrated and hand-lettered, it made my heart do a little dance. I was fascinated that people were creating art in their *Bibles. What a fantastic way to learn Scripture and practice my hand-lettering skills*, I thought.

The concept is not new. Think of the illuminated Bibles that came out of the Romanesque period, where gifted artists poured out their talents and their time to enhance the written text with beautiful pictures. Each book was a unique work of art. Similarly, Bible journaling is a way you and I can use art to enhance our connection with the Word of God.

For a believer, art is an act of worship. You're able to use your God-given creativity and talents to bring honor to Him. Maybe your talent is drawing illustrations or creating landscapes or portraits in the pages. Maybe you're a fantastic hand-letterer and you focus on the words. Maybe you love watercoloring, so you create beautiful colored backgrounds and paintings. Whatever your talent, whatever your skill level, you can create art in your Bible, and it can be an act of worship for you.

It's exciting and inspiring to fill your Bible with art, to look back at those pages and reflect. I hope it encourages you to read a little further and dig in a little more.

Tools

There's an infinite amount of supplies you could bring to this activity. I've listed my most-used, favorite tools to help you. But I would be disappointed to hear that you got overwhelmed and didn't start Bible journaling because you didn't have all the supplies. All you really need is a Bible and a pencil or a pen to do this. I didn't go out and buy all these supplies at once; I accumulated them over time. There's nothing wrong with using what you have and buying a little at a time. **Bible journaling shouldn't break the bank.**

Listed below are my favorite supplies. I starred my top five "Must Haves."

1. **Matte Gesso:** This helps decrease wrinkling and bleed-through because it coats your paper and forms a barrier on the page. It's not a "must-have," but it is helpful if you're

worried about those things. Note: Make sure you purchase a transparent formula, not an opaque one. The package label will tell you which one it is.

2. **Paints:** Pick up an inexpensive palette of watercolors or bottles of acrylic paints at your local craft store. I like a watercolor set with a lot of colors, but you can always mix shades to get different color combinations.

3. **Brushes:** A couple of inexpensive brushes from your local craft store is all you need. Look for multiple sizes—a large round tip and a small round tip, for example. This will help you cover large areas as well as paint fine details.

4. **Ruler:** This is a must if your straight lines are challenged like mine.

5. **Washi:** These Japanese tapes are similar to masking tape and are now easy to find in big box stores as well as craft stores. You can reposition the tape if needed, and they're fun for adding color and decoration to your page—or your pens, or anything else you can imagine—without leaving residue!

6. ***Colored Pencils:** My favorites are Crayola Twistables because they're soft and don't require sharpening. You can find colored pencils anywhere school supplies are sold.

7. ***Fine-Line Pens:** You have several options when it comes to archival ink pens. Microns are the standard for most artists, but there are other strong brands like Staedtler and Tombow that make fine-line pens. They all come in different tip sizes. My favorites are the .01, .03, and .05 sizes. They are waterproof and bleed-proof.

8. ***Calligraphy Brush-Pen:** If you want to do some brush calligraphy in your Bible, my favorite pick is the Tombow Fudenosuke (hard or soft tip). The tip is small enough for your Bible, and it doesn't bleed. At this time you can find them online.

9. **White Gel Pen:** A white gel pen can be used for enhancing your lettering. The paint-like ink will sit on top of the paper and allow your work to pop off the page.

10. ***Pencil:** Any ol' pencil will do! The best pencil is the one you have in hand, right? Or refer to the supply list in chapter 1 for my favorites.

11. Eraser

12. Bookmarks: These fun little embellishments are pretty and help you find your journaling pages more easily. Cut paper tabs or loop some ribbon around a paper clip to make your own.

13. Paper Towel: Keep a couple on hand for spills or watercolor mistakes.

14. *Bible: The Bible I use is the Crossway Books Journaling Bible (ESV double column).

Not all journaling Bibles are created equal—meaning, some papers are thinner than others. Your best bet would be to go to your local Christian bookstore and see what they have. Feel the papers to compare.

Getting Started

Your Bible pages can be elaborate or simple. Try not to get caught up in making your pages look like someone else's. Remember, God made you uniquely you with a creative fingerprint, so be yourself. Pray and ask God to inspire you and help you put away any comparison trap you may be struggling with. And then start.

You may choose to do a simple lettered illustration in black ink—pretty and classic.

If you want to use paint and you're not sure where to start, the following steps illustrate the basic process I like to use:

1. Choose a verse (see sidebar on page 146 for how to shorten long verses if you need help). Think about which words you want to emphasize and what objects

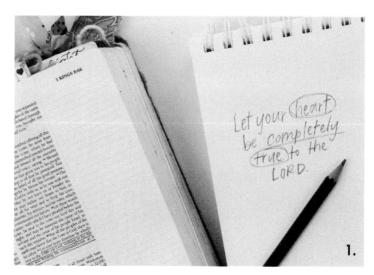

Choosing a Journaling Bible

Choosing a Bible can be overwhelming. Because of the popularity of Bible journaling, there are new creative Bibles being published every year, so your options keep growing. I personally own three different journaling Bibles, each unique in their features. Here are some considerations you should make when you're choosing which Bible to purchase for yourself:

1. *What version do you prefer?* Some people still prefer the King James Version. Others are fond of a paraphrase like the Message. Even more are somewhere in between with the English Standard Version or the New International Version. The good news is, regardless of which version you prefer, there's probably a journaling Bible for you. If this is the most important feature to you, it will narrow your choices considerably.

2. *What is your creative comfort level?* Do you want to create your own artwork in the margins, or do you prefer to color pre-drawn illustrations? You can find many coloring Bibles on the market that mix pre-drawn pages with blank pages, giving you some flexibility. This takes the pressure off if you prefer to color, but do be aware that the pre-drawn pages limit where you can create your own artwork.

3. *Additionally, if you want to create your own artwork but you don't like being limited to a two-inch margin,* there is an interleaved journaling Bible with full-sized blank pages in between each printed page. This allows ample room for notes or art or whatever your creative heart desires.

4. *Before you buy a Bible,* I recommend you take a trip to your local bookstore and physically touch the journaling Bibles they have in stock. Not all Bible paper is created equal, so give the pages a feel and compare a few editions to make sure you know what you're getting. A Bible is an investment that you want to last for years.

5. *The Bibles pictured are: The ESV Journaling Bible* by Crossway Books, *The Message Canvas Bible* by Tyndale, and *The ESV Journaling Bible, Interleaved Edition* by Crossway Books.

you could draw to go with it. In this example, I'm not sure whether I want to use the word "wholly" or "completely." I circled the words I might want to call out.

2. Prepare your paper with a light coat of gesso if you choose.

2.

pro TIP Be careful to hold the edges of your paper so the brushing motion doesn't accidentally wrinkle the page. Note: the edges might curl up a little, but once you close your Bible, they will flatten out.

Painting in Your Bible

Acrylic and watercolor are completely different mediums and should be handled as such when used.

Acrylic paint is thick and opaque. Surprisingly, it doesn't bleed through Bible pages. It will, however, cover up your lettering or the biblical text unless you water it down. Mix a little bit of water with paint in a small paint palette until it's at the transparency you prefer. Oftentimes the color will remain bright even though you can see through it.

Watercolor is a very light and translucent medium, so it won't blot out the words on the page.

pro TIP If you make a mistake when watercoloring, use a dry paper towel and press hard on the paper. Much of the color will lift up. Also note that when the paper dries, the color will end up much lighter than you might expect. Painting in your Bible is fun! I suggest you try both paint options, and don't be afraid to use them together on the same page.

3. Lightly pencil in the verse in a simple skeleton form.

4. With pencil again, go back and fill out the letters in the style you want. Add any flourishes or embellishments you choose.

5. Ink the design with a waterproof pen. Note: If you're unsure whether a pen is waterproof, test it out on a scrap piece and brush water onto it. If the ink smears, it's not waterproof. Be careful when putting watercolor over it.

6. Erase the pencil marks. Note: If you paint over the pencil marks, the paint will coat the paper and make it hard or impossible to erase the pencil afterward.

7. Add color with colored pencils, markers, paints, or a combination of these. If you use paint, allow time for the paint to dry. A hair dryer or heat gun will make it dry faster.

8. Add washi tape and any extra embellishments you want. I love making paper tabs and bookmarks or using stickers and gift tags for added texture, details, and interest.

8.

9. Date it so you can remember when you did it. It's also fun to see how you improve over time!

How to Shorten Long Verses

I have a deep respect for God's Word. But often the sentences are long and it's hard to letter an abundance of words, especially in a small margin. So how do you cut it down but keep the essence of what it's saying? How do you handle it with integrity?

Start with determining the main idea. Understand the overarching message of what the verse is saying. Now say it shorter. Can you pull out a phrase that gives the idea you want to hand-letter?

Here are some examples:

"But if not." I'm inspired by the faith of Shadrach, Meshach, and Abednego and their trust in God, even if they don't get the outcome they hope for. I can't letter the entire passage, but I want to emphasize the part that always challenges me. **The full text is there for me to refer to later.**

"Abide in me and bear much fruit."

The actual passage I wanted to call attention to is quite long—three verses, to be exact. So I kept the main gist for my artwork and, again, the full text is there for me to reference.

How to Prevent Bleeding and Crinkling

Bleed-through and crinkled paper are the hazards of Bible journaling. It's something you should expect and not get too upset about when it happens. But there are a few things you can do to lessen the occurrences:

1. When you're painting, place a piece of plastic under the Bible page you're working on. This will keep the paint from spreading to the edges or bleeding onto the page below. You can use a plastic freezer bag or a laminated piece of paper.

2. Use gesso on your page, as mentioned in the tools section. It's an extra step, but it creates a barrier between the paper and the ink and aids in bleed-through and the crinkled paper.

3. Use less water when you watercolor. The more water you apply to the page, the more it will crinkle and bleed. Start off by going easy on the water. Expect that your paper will crinkle some, but once it's dry and you close your Bible, it will flatten out a good bit.

4. Always test out new markers on the back pages first. Certain kinds of markers will bleed significantly, and you'll want to avoid those.

Ultimately, don't get too caught up in the perfection of it. You're going to mess up, you're going to get some bleeds and crinkles, and you might even tear your page a little. But it's okay. Power through.

jessica smith
1783 CHERRY LN.
TAMPA, FLORIDA 38134

Section 5

Lettering with a Purpose

give
us
THIS DAY
our
DAILY
BREAD
Crayo
AN-DU-SEPTIC
ANTI-DUS
CHALI
12 Nontoxic
White
Chalk

Lifestyle Lettering

Sharing Your Art with Others

Scripture has the power to give life and joy. When you share Scripture verses with a friend, you're sharing life-giving words. In our crazy world, with the news getting darker and more depressing each day, we need to share God's hope and joy more than ever!

When you make and give Scripture art to someone, it is a very special gift. In this chapter, I'll show you a variety of ways to create Scripture art to share with friends. Use these examples as inspiration to launch your creativity!

Anxiety weighs down the heart,
but a kind word cheers it up.

PROVERBS 12:25 NIV

155

1. Greeting Card

Paper cards are still a thing, believe it or not! A greeting card is the simplest and most inexpensive way to share Scripture with a friend. A Scripture verse on the outside and a kind note on the inside is easy to do and can have a big impact.

Tools Needed

- Letter-sized cardstock or watercolor paper
- Pencil/Eraser
- Ruler
- Choice of pens, markers, or paint

Fold the letter-size cardstock in half and cut it to make two 8.5" x 5.5" pieces of paper. Now you have two cards to work with. This is an A2-sized (4.25" x 5.5") card, fitting the standard A2 envelope found in most office stores.

Now, using your imagination, hand-letter a Scripture on the front of your card or water-color a light background first and then letter overtop. You can easily copy from a previously designed verse using a light pad or the window technique mentioned on page 123.

Finish your card with a kind note to your friend. Put your new knowledge to work by addressing the envelope in a special way! Use banners or flowers or calligraphy to turn a boring envelope into something your friend will want to keep.

2. Scripture Print

A simple, inexpensive way to bless a friend is to create a custom Scripture print as a gift. A Scripture print is a great idea to celebrate a wedding, a new baby, a new home, or just because!

Tools Needed

- Letter-sized cardstock
- Pencil/Eraser
- Pen
- Ruler
- Frame (optional)

Draw a bounding box on your paper in the correct size for your finished piece (5″ x 7″ and 8″ x 10″ are standard frame sizes). Hand-letter a Scripture on the front of your card using the tips and techniques you learned in chapters 2–8.

You can use watercolors, markers, colored pencils, etc., to add color if you choose. I love colorful artwork, but I also am drawn to classic black-and-white. You can't go wrong!

Pop your custom Scripture print in a frame and it's ready to go!

3. Bible Memory Cards

Since Scripture memory is an important part of the Christian faith, what better way to encourage a friend than to give her Scripture cards for a unique situation in her life? Better yet, make an extra set for yourself and memorize them together!

Tools Needed

- Set of gift tags (from a craft store)
- Your pen of choice
- Ribbon or baker's twine

Choose five to ten verses and write one verse per card.

Finish off your cards with a ribbon or baker's twine to bundle them together.

4. Chalkboard Sign

I don't know anyone who doesn't like a chalkboard sign even just a little bit. Chalkboards are the perfect way to bring some custom signage to a party, give as a gift, or decorate your home for a holiday. Get creative with the occasions you can use as an excuse to gift a chalkboard sign!

Chalkboards come in a variety of sizes. You can usually find chalkboard door signs or framed boards at a local craft store.

pro-TIP You can make your own chalkboard using a picture frame and a can of chalkboard paint! Use the paint to turn the glass into a chalkboard. Brilliant!

Tools Needed

Note: Your tools will differ depending on the kind of chalkboard project you're doing.

- Chalkboard
- Chalk (my favorite is Crayola Anti-Dust Chalk)
- Pencil sharpener
- Ruler
- Chalk marker* (optional)

*For a gift, a chalk marker might be a better way to go so you don't accidentally smudge the final result. Note: Chalk markers are for nonporous surfaces, which makes them better for vinyl chalkboard material (which has a slick surface). Always test out your chalk marker in an unobtrusive spot to make sure it will erase with water.

First things first: Sharpen your chalk with the pencil sharpener. Yes, that's right. It makes all the difference to have a sharp point on your chalk. The normal blunt edge of chalk simply doesn't allow you to get detailed or precise in your lettering.

Use your ruler to chalk in some guides for your words.

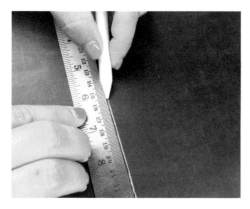

Use the skills and tools you've learned in this book to hand-letter a verse or a phrase for your sign. Use a cotton swab to erase your mistakes as well as your guides when you're finished.

Now you're ready to present your chalkboard gift to the recipient!

5. Custom Notebook/Journal

For a fellow paper-loving friend, find a plain, kraft-covered notebook and custom-draw a design on the front. You can use acrylic paint, a gel pen (shown), or any other material you wish!

Tools Needed:

- Small notebook with a blank cover
- Pencil/Eraser
- Lettering tools of your choice like markers, gel pens, paints, etc.

Great Go-To Scripture Encouragement

1. Romans 8:28

2. Jeremiah 29:11

3. Psalm 23

4. Psalm 18:2

5. 1 Peter 5:7

6. 2 Corinthians 5:7

7. James 4:8

8. Colossians 3:23

9. Joshua 1:9

10. Proverbs 3:5

11. Psalm 1

12. 1 Chronicles 16:11

13. Psalm 40:3

14. Psalm 94:19

15. James 1:5

16. Philippians 4:7

17. Psalm 94:18

18. 2 Corinthians 12:9

19. Psalm 145:18

20. Romans 11:33

Paper Decisions

1. Marker Paper: thin and ultra-smooth. Great for pens and markers to render an inked drawing.

2. Watercolor Paper (hot-pressed and cold-pressed): Thick, textured paper that absorbs water well. Cold-pressed paper is heavily textured and available in notepads and as single pages. Hot-pressed paper is smoother but hard to find. Try looking at a specialty art store if you want to try it.

3. Mixed-Media Paper: Mixed media is a textured paper with a medium thickness that is generally good for wet or dry media, including watercolor, acrylic, colored pencil, marker, pen, pencil, etc. This is a good starter paper if you want to try out a variety of supplies and techniques.

4. Bristol Smooth: This is a great paper for producing a nice finished piece to give to someone. It's thick and smooth, so it's perfect for pen and marker artwork.

5. Cardstock: Believe it or not, your average printer cardstock is a great paper for lettering projects, and it's inexpensive. If you can, look for a paper that says "smooth" on the packaging, or physically touch the paper to find one that feels the smoothest.

6. Miscellaneous Projects

Other creative projects you can use your lettering skills for:

Gift Tags

Place Cards

School Signs

Pallet Signs

He who dwells in the shelter of the MOST HIGH will Abide IN THE SHADOW OF THE Almighty

PSALM 91:1 #LetterfortheLORD

Lettering for the Lord

Dealing with Creative Insecurities

*T*his chapter is less about growing your skills and more about freeing your heart. You might feel overwhelmed by what you've learned in this book and have yet to put into practice.

You're not alone in your fears and insecurities. This is a struggle for all creatives, and it doesn't go away as our skills get better. There will always be someone further along or more talented than you. You will always compare yourself to someone else.

Confession: I'm often plagued with doubts and fears about my lettering ability or sharing my work with the world. I've also suffered from comparison disease, where I feel that my efforts and my work don't match my expectations.

So what is a creative heart to do?

Soli Deo Gloria

S.D.G. That's what two of the world's greatest composers, Johann Sebastian Bach and George Frideric Handel, both born in Germany in 1685, inscribed at the bottom of their works. It means "To God alone be the glory."

Bach declared that the aim and final end of all music should be none other than the glory of God and the refreshment of the soul. I would echo Bach that the aim and final end of all *creative work* should be none other than the glory of God and the refreshment of the soul.

Let's not forget why we're here on earth, living this life, doing this thing called art. Bach and Handel created for the sake of praising God and bringing glory to Him. The phrase should remind us that we're not here for our own glory or fame.

Art should be done to make much of Him. Your life, your very breath, is to bring glory and honor to the Lord. Doesn't that change the meaning of what you're doing right now? Laundry? Cleaning up after a sick child? Working for an inconsiderate boss? All these things we are to do in a way that brings glory to God. This is a mind-set shift.

So how do we bring this mind-set shift into our creative world in a practical way? Let's explore some of the feelings of overwhelmedness, discouragement, and jealousy that accompany creatives the world over and see how we can rise above them.

If we were sitting at a table over coffee together, this is what I would share with you.

Overcoming the Perfection Mentality

I see you, afraid to start drawing in your Bible because you don't want to ruin it. I see you, trying hard to hand-letter but always feeling disappointed with the end result. I see you, scrolling on social media and feeling that twinge of jealousy that you didn't create like someone else. I see you because I am that way too.

Women frequently tell me, "I'm afraid to start because I don't want to mess up!" I get that. I do. And I think, *That's sad.* Because what's the point of Bible journaling if you aren't willing to mess it up a little? Art is messy. Life is messy. Jesus wasn't afraid of messes. He encountered them everywhere He went.

Let me tell you something else. Perfection isn't real. In fact, "pretty and perfect" often means "plastic and fake." That certainly isn't you. You are real and lovely, and you have a story to tell. And just like you, a journaled Bible or a messy, coffee-spilled prayer journal tells a story. Your story. **It's beautiful, worn, and lived in, and it speaks to your journey and your worship and your love for the Lord.**

My journaling Bible is literally taped together at the binding—what can I say? I'm rough on books. My prayer journal has coffee stains on it and scribbles from my kids who picked up a pen and wrote on it when I was out of the room. My sermon notebook is full of spelling errors, mistakes, and not-so-pretty lettering.

God isn't less glorified in your imperfection.

Even with all these mistakes and messes, God's Word is being consumed. These incomplete, imperfect projects point to the time you spent with Him, worshiping with your art and using the talent He gave you.

God intends His holy Scriptures to be nestled within your heart and lived out.

Recognize that the art expressions coming from your prayer and Bible-study times are inspired, one-of-a-kind worship that only you can give. **That art has flaws and mistakes, but it is more beautiful because it's genuine and authentic.**

If fear of messing up is your problem, pray and ask God to help you overcome that. And then determine to just start.

Avoiding the Comparison Trap

I've always compared my ability to someone one step ahead of me. It doesn't matter how much I improve; I'm always looking at someone more advanced. It's terribly discouraging, and there are days I consider giving up. Does that sound familiar? You'll never get creatively inspired from that kind of mind-set. If you're caught up in the comparison trap, you'll sink deeper and deeper into this insecurity until you start avoiding the creative process altogether.

I speak from a place of experience.

Six months after I tentatively started selling my artwork online, I hit a wall. Debilitating fear of putting myself out there consumed me. I'd wake up every morning and spend hours consuming other people's blog posts and social-media feeds, and I'd despair that I could never pull myself together to be that good or do what they were doing.

I was never happy with what I made, and so I began avoiding the creative process altogether. I threw myself into other projects. Yes, I emerged with a nicely organized home, but God used this time to expose my insecurities and force me to identify what I was avoiding.

I believe our insecurity comes from putting too much emphasis on our personal abilities rather than **God's ability to use our work.** You start living in your own strength instead of in the strength of the One who made you creative in the first place. You place a critical eye on your perceived lack of ability and then you're never happy with what you do. You can't continue like that. If comparison has become a problem for you, start asking God to help you put blinders on so you can create for His glory alone.

Your story is what God is doing through you, the desires He puts in your heart. Maybe you want to create art and be paid for it. Maybe you simply want to connect with Him on a deeper level in your own spiritual walk. Maybe you want to use your gifts and talents to bless someone in your life. Either way, recognize that God has given you special abilities, dreams, and desires. Keep doing what God puts in front of you.

Defeating the Idea that You're Not Creative

Men and women alike will tell me, "I'm not creative, but I always wished I was!" I've begun to realize that they are basing their definition of "creative" on artistic ability alone. To them, being creative means they have to be able to produce fine art or draw a certain way. Can you relate to this feeling? I believe the enemy has sold you a lie. He says, "You're not creative (in a formal, artistic sense)"; therefore, you don't have permission to try creative things.

In reality, being creative means using your imagination to create or solve. If you identify creativity as specifically artistic, you're completely missing the idea that God gave you a *unique brand of creativity*. The word *creative* is defined as "having good imagination or original ideas." See? Nothing about artistic skill.

Remember, you have creativity woven into your DNA because you, dear friend, were made in the image of Creator God (Genesis 1:27). You were born creative. That creativity comes in many forms and functions. You can live creatively without loads of artistic ability. And artistic skills can also be developed. Be assured, we're not all meant to create the same way. How boring would that be?

The enemy wants you to believe you're not creative and therefore you *can't*. He wants you to feel "less than," rather than empowered by the Creator to do good works (which God planned in advance for you to do, Ephesians 2:10). He wants you to sell yourself short and allow this attitude to shape who you are.

Ask God to help you embrace the style of creativity He's given you. Ask Him to help you experience the power and the change it can have on your life. Don't wait for someone else to give you permission, for He put that desire in you when He created you.

The next time the enemy whispers in your ear that you're not capable of being creative, go to the Source of all creative endeavors and ask Him to endue you with His creativity.

Letter for the Lord

The idea of lettering for the Lord came to me when I read the words David penned in Psalm 51:15, "Open my lips, that my mouth may declare Your praise" (NASB). I was still very new to hand-lettering, and I thought, *If every time David opened his mouth, he wished to declare the praises of God, then likewise every time I use my pen, I want it to declare the praises of God.* I committed then and there, "Lord, if You'll let me hand-letter, I will use it for Your glory." I began posting to social media what God was teaching me, and I used the hashtag #letterfortheLord. It took the pressure off. It helped me post hand-lettered verses even when I cringed at the imperfection of them. It gave me joy to know that I was using my

And WE know THAT GOD causes all things TO WORK for GOOD to those WHO love Him
romans 8:28

creative gifts for the glory of the Lord regardless of what other people thought. Over time, I noticed others were using the hashtag too.

When you "Letter for the Lord," you're not lettering for other people. You're not posting for your own glory or popularity. Whether it brings you likes or comments or not, that is not the goal. It's about not getting caught up in what other people think of you.

I don't mean to convey that I do this perfectly. There are plenty of times when I worry about what people will say in my comments. It's okay to feel a little uncomfortable. Playing it safe will never stretch you.

With the rise of social media, our society is becoming more and more self-centered. Lettering for the Lord is a serious change of mind-set. Do it to bring glory to HIS name. Share His goodness, His truth, His hope to the world. **When you create from this point of authenticity and share what God has done in your life, you're honoring Him above yourself.** And I believe God honors that.

What if you were to write *S.D.G.* on the bottom of all your creations? Would it change the way you view it? Will you allow God to use you right now, wherever you are, with the current state of your ability?

He invites us to join Him. We can share in the blessing of boldly spreading His great name.

> *Whatever you do, work at it with your whole being, for the Lord and not for men, because you know that you will receive an inheritance from the Lord as your reward. It is the Lord Christ you are serving*
> *(Colossians 3:23–24 BSB).*

*D*rawing from more than ten years of graphic design experience, KRYSTAL WHITTEN has cultivated a large following of creatives on Instagram who have embraced her unique combination of lettering and faith. Through her social media, speaking engagements, and in-person workshops she unites her love for God's Word with her passion for hand lettering, inspiring believers to go deeper in their faith by getting more interactive with their Bibles. Krystal is the creator of *The Lettering Prayer Journal, Faith & Lettering Journal,* and launched her stationery and gift line in summer 2017. She lives in Land O'Lakes, Florida with her husband, Andy, and two children, Pierce and Haven.

Follow Krystal online for more pro-tips and inspiration: KrystalWhitten.com

 @KrystalWhitten

post your images!

SHARE ON SOCIAL MEDIA USING
#faithandlettering #letterfortheLord

Want more room to practice and hone your lettering skills? Get the companion journal!

Available wherever books are sold.